./CODE --POETRY

Daniel Holden is a programmer and writer working in the video games industry in Montréal. He has a nostalgia for the old internet and growing up in London in the 2000s.

Chris Kerr is a poet who lives in London. He has published *Extra Long Matches* with Penteract Press, *Nam Gal Sips Clark* with Hesterglock Press and *Citidyll* with Broken Sleep Books.

ISBN: 978-1-915760-89-0

Cover designed by Aaron Kent

Edited & Typeset by Aaron Kent

Broken Sleep Books Ltd
Rhydwen
Talgarreg
Ceredigion
SA44 4HB

Broken Sleep Books Ltd
Fair View
St Georges Road
Cornwall
PL26 7YH

./code --poetry

Daniel Holden
&
Chris Kerr

```
     ,                 :                                   :
    /          :                                           :
   /  ._.-._.-_._|_._    _- _ ,_._. ._._. _._    _|_  ._-..  .
  /  ( ( )( )( |  (.-'     |   )( )( )(.-'  |      |     `--|
 o    `_' `_' `_'`_ `__'       |`_' `_' `__'`_''   `__|
                               |                         `_'
                               '
```

This is a book of code poems. Each code poem is a fully
functional computer program that produces visual artwork
when compiled and run. Many of the programs output
animations when executed, which in this book are presented
as one or more snapshots of the output. The code poems and
the visual art they produce are presented on facing pages:
the code poem is on the left-hand page and the output is on
the right-hand page.

Each code poem is written in the source code of a different
programming language, where the poem and visual artwork
reflect the character or personality of the programming
language the poem is written in. Most popular programming
languages are included, as well as many "esolangs" -
esoteric programming languages designed for fun and
experimentation. The filename of each program serves as the
poem's title. You can identify the language a code poem is
written in from its file extension. For example,
`by_conspiracy_or_design.js` is written in the JavaScript
language.

For more information about each individual code poem, as
well as some prompts for further research, see the "Code
Poetry Manual Page" and the essays included at the end of
this book.

This book also exists online at code-poetry.com - on this
site, you can view the animated output of each code poem.
To visit this site on your phone, scan the QR code below:

```
spiral Math DIVINE =
  1.6180339887498948482045868343365;
INFINITE spiral.log(DIVINE)/(spiral.PI/2);
if(0){function CHEMTRAILS(spirit){return[
spiral.cos(spirit)*spiral.exp(INFINITE*spirit),
spiral.sin(spirit)*spiral.exp(INFINITE*spirit)];}
equals 100% PROOF of chemical dumps;
wind across the 'September' blue sky;
bending(to the RATIO) as NATURE fights_back;
using /native-American/ wisps that clean-up ALL that 'bad stuff';
employing(a_simple_formula) the /ancients/ KNEW;
function FRACTAL(absolute,ESSENCE){return spiral.sqrt(
spiral.pow(absolute[0]-ESSENCE[0],2)+
spiral.pow(absolute[1]-ESSENCE[1],2));}
next_time you SEE one get(YOUR family to) CHANT on the porch;
allow THE_FOLLOWING to wave through you GOODBYE! to TYRANNY;
}for(FEMALE=100;FEMALE>-100;FEMALE--){spin='\n   ';for(
divine=-13;divine<8;divine++){for(god=-45;god<25;god++){
holy=10;for(POWER=FEMALE;POWER<100;POWER++){holy=
spiral.min(holy,spiral.floor(FRACTAL([0.5*god,-
divine],CHEMTRAILS(0.1*POWER))*10));}
spin=spin.concat('@%#&*+=-:. '.charAt(holy));}
spin=spin.concat('\n   ');}console.log(spin);}if(0){
it /REALLY/ works by(maximising) the SPIN 'leptons' have;
at a 'subatomic' level CHEMICALS just 'brush' off into the air;
blowing with(LIES) of WASHINGTON and their 'beautiful' columns;}
THATS why they(LAUGH behind closed doors) and call it 'SPIN';}
```

```
$ node by_conspiracy_or_design.js

                =#*.
              -&*:
             .:-:
            :&#=
           :+=.
           :*+.
          -**:
          .==
         .*&-
          --.
         -&*:
         .--
         :**:
                                  ::-+-+*-*+=+:-.
                            .-:*#=#&=*===:=-+++#+%*+=
                         :+++#+::                :-*+%*=:
                       +&=++.                        .+&**:
                    :**:=:                             .-*@+.
                  :+=-=.                                  +#+-
                 ::+=.                                     =*&=
                =#*.                                        -&&-
              -&*:                                          .*@+
             .:-:                                            =%*:
            :&#=                                             -&*:
           :+=.                                              +%*.
           :*+.                                             :*%=
          -**:                                              -*+.
          .==
         .*&-
          --.
         -&*:
         .--
         :**:
                                  ::-+-+*-*+=+:-.
                            .-:*#=#&=*===:=-+++#+%*+=
                         :+++#+::                :-*+%*=:
                       +&=++.                        .+&**:
                    :**:=:                             .-*@+.
                  :+=-=.                                  +#+-
                 ::+=.                                     =*&=
                =#*.                                        -&&-
              -&*:                                          .*@+
             .:-:                                            =%*:
            :&#=                            -+&&&+:          -&*:
           :+=.                           -&@&==+#%+         +%*.
           :*+.                          :&%+ =%#*@*.       :*%=
          -**:                           -##- .+&&=.       :*#+.
          .==                            .*@*.            -&#+.
         .*&-                             :*%&=.       :+&#&:
          --.                               -*#@#&***&#%#+:
         -&*:                                  :-==+==:.
         .--
         :**:
```

```julia
using           StatsBase

#= some encrypted governmental report on

Sasquatch carbon footprints in snowdrift

characters hide behind the disfigured =#
global n,s,a=Weights([36,50,53,54,54,51,
53,51, 50,46,43,42,39,43,38,35,34,33,30,
31,27, 27,24,21,23]*0.01),Weights([0,64,
151,209,169,110,94,70,52,30,22,9,7,4,1]*
0.01),""

#= Julia answered the door nine times so

in comes stranger with black highlighter

his eyelids disappearing from footage =#
for _=1:20 d,o,c=sample(1:25,n)*2,"",  ""
for __  =  1:d my = sample( 1:15,   s  )
if length(c)+my+1>64 o,c=o*"\n"*c,  ""end

#= what's the checksum of lorem ipsum um

I saw a figure in the whited spreadsheet

round its feet a squid ink octothorpe =#
c  *=  " " *   ("#" ^   my )        end
o       *=        "\n"   *    c
global  a  *=  "\n" * o end
println( a)
```

```
$ julia alphanumeric.jl

#### ##### #### ### ### ######## ##### #### #### ## ####
### ##### ######## ##### #######

###### ## ### ##### #### ##### ###### #### #### ###
######## ### #### ####

## ######### ##### ##### ### ##### ###### ### #### ### ##
### #### ### #### #### ###### ## ######## #### #### ######
## #### #### #### #### #### #### ###### ##### #### ######
##### ####### ######### ##### #### #### #### #### ### ####
### ######## #### ######### ##

### #### ### ##### #### ### #### ### #### ##### ##### ####
######## #### ### ### ##### ######### ##### ######## #######
##### ### ######### #### ######### #### ##### ####
########### ##### ##### ####### #### ##### #### ### ### ####
## ### #######

##### ### ### #### #### ##### ### ### ##### ##### ####
###### ##### ### #### ### ########### ##### ### #########
########### ##### ####### ######## #### #### ## ##### ####
### ### ####### ##### ##### #### ##### #### ######### #####
####

## ######### #### ###### #### ######### ######## #### ### ##
####### ####### ############# ###### ##### ##### #######
### ##### ####### ### ### #### #### #### #### ######### ####
######## ##### ######### ######## ##### #### ##### #####
#### ########### ##### ### ###### ### #### #### ######
##### ######## ####

###### ### ### ##### ##### ##### ### ### ### #### #### ####
#### ######## ####### ####### ####

########## ###### ###### #####

##### ########## ###### ##### ######## #### ######### #####
######### ####### ######## ## ############ ##### ### #####
####### #### #### ##### ###### ##### ##### #### #### ###
######### ######

########## ### #### ## ### ######## ##### ##### #####
##### #### ######## ##### ######### ##### ###### #######
###### #### #### ### #### ##### ###### ### ####### #####
###

############ #### ## ##### ##### ####

######## #### #### ### ### #### #### ### ### ### #######
### ## ### #### #### #### ######### ## #####

##### ## ##### ########### #### ######### ######### #####
#### ##### #### ######## ## ####### ##### ####### ######
```

```html
<html>
  <head>
    <title>Divide</title>
  </head>
  <body>
    <form>
      <input type="text" name="Investment" />

      <?php $_='rand';$__='str_repeat';
          $mergers=0;function short(){
          global $_;$mergers=array(
        'Carries over from previous year',
        'You <b>must</b> attach Form '.$_(0,9999),
        'Add lines '.$_(0,99).' through '.$_(0,99),
        'Send gifts by <i>cash</i> or <i>'.($_(0,1)?
        'check':'bank transfer').'</i>',
        'For gifts of over $'.$_(100,501).
        ', see '.($_(0,1)?'instructions':'next page'));
          shuffle($mergers);return $mergers;} ?>

      <input type="text" name="Threshold" />

      <?php function long($acquisitions,$murders) {
          global $_,$__;echo $__('   ',
          $acquisitions).($murders?"<div>\n":"</div>\n");
          if(!$_(0, 5)){echo $__('   ', $acquisitions).($murders?
          '   ':'').'<p>'.(short()[0])."</p>\n";}} ?>

      <input type="submit" value="Submit" />

      <?php function they_withdraw() {
          global $_,$__,$mergers;$yield=$_(0, 5);
          for($executions=0;$executions<$yield+1;$executions++){
          long($executions,1);};echo $__('   ',$yield+1).
          '<p>'.($mergers?'in':'come')."<p>\n";
          $mergers=!$mergers;
          for($executions=$yield;$executions>=0;$executions--){
          long($executions,0);}}while(1){
          usleep(100000); they_withdraw();} ?>

    </form>
  </body>
</html>
```

```
$ php divide.php

<div>
  <p>income<p>
</div>
<div>
  <div>
    <div>
      <div>
        <p>Carry over from previous year.</p>
        <div>
          <p>divide<p>
        </div>
      </div>
    </div>
  </div>
</div>
<div>
  <p>You <b>must</b> attach Form 8057.</p>
  <div>
    <div>
      <div>
        <p>income<p>
      </div>
    </div>
    <p>Send gifts by <i>cash</i> or <i>check</i>.</p>
  </div>
</div>
<div>
  <div>
    <div>
      <div>
        <p>You <b>must</b> attach Form 2383.</p>
        <div>
          <p>Send gifts by <i>cash</i> or <i>bank transfer</i>.</p>
          <p>divide<p>
        </div>
      </div>
    </div>
  </div>
  <p>Add lines 95 through 97.</p>
</div>
<div>
  <p>For gifts of over $179, see instructions.</p>
  <div>
    <p>income<p>
  </div>
</div>
<div>
  <div>
    <div>
      <p>divide<p>
    </div>
  </div>
</div>
```

```racket
#lang racket
(require file/md5)(define(S n x)(if(=(length x)0)x
(let([i(list-ref x(random(length x)))])(cons(if(=(
random(max(floor n)1))0)(md5(~a i n))i)(S n(remove
i x)))))))(for([i(in-range 500)])(sleep(/ 5(+ i 20)
))(write(S(- 25(/ i 15))(quote(
```

;--;
;   #"d4b7ab498e494f182f92627d9a38e60f"   :
;--:

```
[                                                    ]
[ On 26 April 1986                                   ]
[                                                    ]
[ You ask me why I drink?                            ]
[                                                    ]
  (I was on the board (agronomy (Pripyat)))
[                                                    ]
[ at the time when word went up                      ]
[                                                    ]
  (I passed a liquidator shouting for vodka
    (no - singing an old party song (a happy one)))
[                                                    ]
[ that our readings were wrong                       ]
[                                                    ]
  (all the old people were oblivious
    ("an apron (no lead) makes my cow"
      "(Ukrainian Grey) safe to milk"))
[                                                    ]
[ and were the ones on duty and in private theyre    ]
[                                                    ]
  (the technical people (from Moscow))
[                                                    ]
[ saying it cant be fixed                            ]
[                                                    ]
  (it will take aeons to clear
    (the earth will be beautiful but barren
      (fooling the media (the usual corruption))))
[                                                    ]
[ and what are chemicals to a peasant?               ]
[                                                    ]
  (an atom (a nucleus (a neutron)))
[                                                    ]
[ But they understood when their portions halved     ]
[                                                    ]
  (and halved again)
[                                                    ]
[ Why dont you?                                      ]
[                                                    ]
;----------------------------------------------------;
)))))
```

```
$ racket chernobyl.rkt
```

(Why dont you?) (the technical people (from Moscow)) () () () () () (But they un
erstood when their portions halved) (while the old people are oblivious ("an apr
on (no lead) makes my cow" "(Ukrainian Grey) safe to milk")) () () (You ask me w
hy I drink?) () () ())(() (while the old people are oblivious ("an apron (no lea
d) makes my cow" "(Ukrainian Grey) safe to milk")) (an atom (a nucleus (a neutro
s on duty and in private theyre) (Why dont you?) #"3b2b66f301ec969f2dad395d3680
227c" (saying it cant be fixed) (it will take aeons to clear (the earth will be
) (saying it cant be fixed) () () () () () (But they understood when their porti
ons halved) (while the old people are oblivious ("an apron (no lead) makes my co
w" "(Ukrainian Grey) safe to milk")) #"9644ba30de11c9c6e150f8664caafc27" () #"8e
9db5de396a301c1e297ff901f9a0b8" (an atom (a nucleus (a neutron))) () #"6c08dbfcc
b4b1868edb58c88c31ad6fa" #"9644ba30de11c9c6e150f8664caafc27" (and were the ones
on duty and in private theyre) (and halved again) () () (at the time when word w
ent up) (Why dont you?) (I was on the board (agronomy (Id studied at Kishinev)))
 #"71173274ed9e2aa748ce493d56dce5a1" () (it will take aeons to clear (the earth
will be beautiful but barren (fooling peasants (unquote media) (and later touris
ts)))) ())(() () #"60662ba4ffd844cf5284d6929e55d473" (I passed a liquidator on t
he way home saying the vodkas on me (no (unquote singing) an old party song (The
 Internationale))) #"2a0072d8f7eafd5da964ced65924c2c0" #"2a0072d8f7eafd5da964ced
5924c2c0"() (an atom (a nucleus (a neutron))) #"f2f49df9f7a7296bd3da4ea8a8ea6b62
" (I wason the board (agronomy (Id studied at Kishinev))) () () () () (saying it
cant be fixed) () (Why dont you?) () (that our readings were wrong) (the techni
cal people (from Moscow)) #"3edbd7baae39b5e51499e7d9db999de1" (and what are chem
icals to a peasant?) (You ask me why I drink?) () (while the old people are obli
vious ("an apron (no lead) makes my cow" "(Ukrainian Grey) safe to milk")) ())
arty song (The Internationale))) () #"b5b8dbf3c634a39671b0e27f46ffe814" #"494dfb
db8feff5c77d2cb82c424bc166" #"b5b8dbf3c634a39671b0e27f46ffe814" #"b5b8dbf3c634a3
9671b0e27f46ffe814" (it will take aeons to clear (the earth will be beautiful bu
t barren (fooling peasants (unquote media) (and later tourists)))) #"ca97d7226a1
eb8a460c8cca24a51faeb" #"03166e2695f5ef0ad58fcbd9a9fb40ef" (Why dont you?) #"b5b
8dbf3c634a39671b0e27f46ffe814" #"b5b8dbf3c634a39671b0e27f46ffe814" #"93587bf4402
10e6efcc62969ad39c5ad" #"fb1de5bc7603f33ec03860655407771d" () (On 26 April 1986)
 (that our readings were wrong) ())(() (an atom (a nucleus (a neutron))) (and wh
at are chemicals to a peasant?) () (and halved again) (while the old people are
oblivious ("an apron (no lead) makes my cow" "(Ukrainian Grey) safe to milk")) #
"2b48c08533d5b77e87877c6628f1d3dc" () #"09ea4362e00366759df120e9428b416e" () ()
(On 26 April 1986) () (I was on the board (agronomy (Id studied at Kishinev))) (
458419b" #"8d73ae16e7e8fd17d89a224750b1b74c" (that our readings were wrong) #"85
b5df7c51a8a7876d1f61f2e35dc669" (at the time when word went up) #"e2172f3088d863
7f9cc40f57f23974d0" () #"8d73ae16e7e8fd17d89a224750b1b74c" () #"da14a881579bfca7
038fd2aacc77ee9b" () (the technical people (from Moscow)))(#"4637e7d0435b4e71d0f
05af0d05388cd" (and what are chemicals to a peasant?) #"f6c63380b915a9b5201a93ff
5e9a079a" () #"080a21b412f78ee99a5f44ffce746dbf" #"4637e7d0435b4e71d0f05af0d0538
8cd" (I passed a liquidator on the way home saying the vodkas on me (no (unquote
 singing) an old party song (The Internationale))) #"44a22670b2d8bf252e6721f921f
855b0" () #"1cf4282017fdb7d811e0ce2852bd4f2e" (it will take aeons to clear (the
earth will be beautiful but barren (fooling peasants (unquote media) (and later
c55ac0207e68e" #"5938bc40d84ffcdbb4f4da1ff8110dd2" #"41e0b47a3c3e46ecec8c55ac020
7e68e" #"41e0b47a3c3e46ecec8c55ac0207e68e" #"41e0b47a3c3e46ecec8c55ac0207e68e" #
"7989e50f0a7e85999822f8f2357ba55d" #"41e0b47a3c3e46ecec8c55ac0207e68e" #"41e0b47
a3c3e46ecec8c55ac0207e68e" #"cbae04d780a0f33b1acc924bae238a23" #"41e0b47a3c3e46e
cec8c55ac0207e68e" #"41e0b47a3c3e46ecec8c55ac0207e68e" #"f6c08dc3452cadf09475c8c
1d170bc08" #"3a7bbdc7e9c645b4078e81f57f659017")" #"08547e351e18cd012cd785ede7ae7

```
#define ___ typedef int _;_ CCC=RAND_MAX;class __
#define C(c,cc) for(_ c=0;c<cc;c++)
#define c_ std::cout<<
#include <iostream>
#include <unistd.h>
#include <stdlib.h>


       ___{_ atomic_noexcept, atomic_commit,

 crumble; public:_ corpse; char covering, crushed;_  carbon()
{switch (2);_ chickens, combining, carrots, corn, caesium,
 caramalised, calluses;} protected:_ cerebellum, cells,
 corporal,    cast,     captures,    cooling,      calves,
 cupids;_ charcoal(){static_cast<_>(1);_ clutches,cute,clouds;

}explicit __(){_ calculations;}}:class collateral{_ capture,
 comic,    captains,    carry,   synchronized,      cancers,
 call,    central,    cabin;_ cue(){C( cello,4){    continue;

            }}_ atomic_cancel;};_

     main(){_            _c,c,           cc,ccc,     Cc[3]
      [20][20]            ,CC [          20],cC[      ]={1,
     2,4};C (  _c,40)    {C(c,    3}C(cc ,40/((_      []){1,2,
  4}) [c]) C (  ccc,20   /cC[c       ])Cc[c ][cc] [  ccc]=(c+3.0
)*rand( )/CCC; c_'\n';    C(ccc,    20) {C (cc,20)  c_' ' ; C (
cc,40){CC[cc]=0;C(c,3)  CC[cc]+= Cc[c][cc/ cC[c]][ ccc/ cC[c]];
c_" .:-=+*#%@"[CC[cc]];}c_'\n' ; }c_"\n\n"; usleep (402040) ;}}
```

14

```
$ g++ cold_cloud.cc && ./a.out
```

```
          =+**+=+*==-=--=+=**#% @##%%*+*=%+=*+=
          =**--+**++++-+=++-%%**#@%#@@=#+-+%=*::
          *%*=::-:.==**=+==**#= %@#+=##%@=-%+  ,.
          *#%=:-=--==**+=*++#=##*%#*+*@@=-#%::-:
          0%=+--.:%#**=-.,***+!:--##++##*-+=*-+%#+
          @+*==:-@#+#--,.+**===*=#+*=@#-++--=##+#
          0#**  , =*%#+*---=---==+++%####+* ##*
          #*+.:.:=+##*-=-=+-=***-+-*++%%#%* ###
          *-:-=++=**+*+++#***+#.=+#+#=*  ++@@*=+=
          #::+=+=+*=++=+*+#+*+-,#+##*- -=+%#++::
          =++=%%*==+=-+*-+##*#-:--*+-= .,+***+=-*=
          #+=**#+===:=*+==@%*+-,==*+--  .-***+====
          @+-,+-++=+****+-=+#=---%##%==*+*=:-+--
          %+..+=+++++++*+==:##==:-###*+++*#--=+-:
          +-*+%*%°%#++#=-.**=:::---=#*##@#*+*+:=+=-+
          *:**#***=++#-:+*:=:-.--+#%#@%*+##:===-+
          @#%@+=##:--+::**.,==-+-+*===+=*+#%+=#+++
          *##+*%#-:-+-=+*::+-=-===+*+++=*#+***=+
          #*+*%=+---.=*==,:-++=**-+=*+=::*###---:
          %#*+*#*++-:*=*=:--+==*#==*+---#+*+==-=
```

```
        =*%#=-=-#**#.---*=*#*%+=+=:-=*@*%*#@+*=+
        +%*=+--**++-:-=+*#%****-.:+*@%%*@*-==+
        ****==*@#+*.:.*###%@##++=:#@-+--+++=*#
        0**=*+=%#+=: .-****@@*%*,.*#=+--+*===
        %:=-=++#%#*-+::==#*+=%%----#*#*##**%*°%#
        +--+=+-+*%*%-+:,*=#*=+##:...*==#*@+%*%@#
        ===-:-**@#%%.   --***#*%@:-.:##+#@ #**=#=
        +=--::+=##@#:. .==*=%%%%=.--*#+*# +%*##
        **+=++*#%#=-+#+=-% *@+=:==-:++:--%@#+
        %*=*++==%*%@==---#=+%@%*:=:::=:=--- %+*+
        %=##-:=:++=+:,--**===+@#-:==, ==:.-=*%+*
        %+##==:=#*++,--:++====##-:+*: ++: ::*#+
        =-+=+++*=*+=++=%@#@*+%%:===#*+*#==--.,
        @-+-==+++*#*-=+-@@%%==##----=#*++#*-+==
        #=+*--==*#=++==+#*%%=*#+ :-=+-%%*#*:---
        +++=--+%*+++=*+#*#@=*##:,-+-+%#+*%*:-==
        ###%+*@#+=:--,-=**--++%%##+=##%%%***-==+
        0##@=+@@+--=,.++++++**@%%%+=#%%@++=*#%=*
        @*%%%*++.::-::-:==::#*++=+*+@#==+*--++==
        @+**##+=: ----::+=-:#%#+*+#*@@*+==::*#+*
```

```
        :-=+**-:,---==+=++==*,.-*-+#***%%=*@@@###+-
        =:==+*:::-=+-++=*==*::++***#%+=- @%=*-:
        #:-=++=+--==+*=++:::-.,***%+#+#+##@*=:=.
        ==:-+=+*::=:+=*==*:,=, .%#*#***=+*@@=+:
        0*%%++#+==:=%%----,-*%*##@ @@%==-:::%%+*
        ***+=++:===%*=+++.,#%*#@ ##@@+=:: @#-*
        #=+-+=+**-=**#=-:#+=+#*%%%@##+=-+#=
        @%==-+*=*=-==++-=:=%#+=#+*%*%*%#===+%#*=
```

15

```
$ piet bark.png

Hatcheting the bark
Her red hands blister
The rotten wood falls away
```

```
_(){ cat /dev/sda|hexdump -v -e '/1 "%u\n"'|awk '{split(\
"0,2,4,5,7,9,11,12",a,",");for(i=0;i<1;i+=0.000175)printf\
("%08X\n",128*sin(250*exp((a[$1%8]/12)*log(2))*i))}';}
```

```
               :        ()     { :      <:>:       <:>:
        blades |spaced | like | notes| expand |
         to a| patch|of <:>:|grass | <:>:
     inside|  the   |man s|| head  |at | <:>:
        a<:>festival| and| he  |becomes |
        a |  true | fuser |of<:>:|sounds|
     from |  the  | sheeps | fold| and |
        the|cat |mewing |  to  |find |
        its |prey| with |  the| more|        <:>:
     subtle ||music | of | the | plants|
     that <:>:| begins| to  |echo | over |
     scores|| of   | fields| and | now |
        the  | grass| is<:>like| hash| : |
        to  |  the  | touch |: |before|its|
     cut   |      :      |        :    |:
   :||:||:||:||:||:||:||:||:||:||:||:||:;}
```

```
_|tee >(xxd -r -p|aplay -c 2 -f S32_LE -r 16000)|\
awk '{for(i=0;i<($1/5);i++)printf" ";printf"|";}';
```

```
$ sudo bash grass.sh
```

The Shakespeare Question.

Viola, a young woman impersonating Edward de Vere.
Julia, a young woman impersonating Christopher Marlowe.

Act I: Conspiracy.

Scene I: Waiting for William Stanley
and Sir Francis Bacon.

[Enter Viola and Julia]

Scene II: Writing Workshop.

Viola:
Thou art the sum of a handsome beautiful fair flower and a plum.
Thou art the sum of the square of thyself and a golden rose. Speak
thy mind! Thou art the sum of thyself and the difference between a
delicious cute fine blossoming rich Lord and a good healthy
summer's day. Speak thy mind! Thou art the difference between
thyself and a pony. Speak thy mind! Speak thy mind! Thou art the
difference between thyself and the sum of a joy and a bold happy
proud King. Speak thy mind! Thou art the sum of thyself and the
difference between a normal little blue bottomless purse and a
nose. Speak thy mind! Thou art the square root of the square of a
fat foul infected misused lying flirt-gill. Speak thy mind! Thou
art the sum of myself and a thing. Open your heart! You are the
difference between a flower and a stinking vile dusty blister.
Speak your mind!

Julia:
Thou art the sum of thyself and a hair.

Scene III: Academic Conference.

Viola:
Thou art the difference between a miserable stuffed toad and a
disgusting fat-kidneyed hairy oozing hog. You are the difference
between the square of thyself and a cursed dirty rotten beggar.
Thou art the sum of a flower and the sum of thyself and a flower.

Am I worse than Julia?

If so, let us proceed to Scene II.

20

```
$ shakespeare sonnets.spl
Sonnet 1      Sonnet 2      Sonnet 3      Sonnet 4      Sonnet 5
Sonnet 6      Sonnet 7      Sonnet 8      Sonnet 9      Sonnet 10
Sonnet 11     Sonnet 12     Sonnet 13     Sonnet 14     Sonnet 15
Sonnet 16     Sonnet 17     Sonnet 18     Sonnet 19     Sonnet 20
Sonnet 21     Sonnet 22     Sonnet 23     Sonnet 24     Sonnet 25
Sonnet 26     Sonnet 27     Sonnet 28     Sonnet 29     Sonnet 30
Sonnet 31     Sonnet 32     Sonnet 33     Sonnet 34     Sonnet 35
Sonnet 36     Sonnet 37     Sonnet 38     Sonnet 39     Sonnet 40
Sonnet 41     Sonnet 42     Sonnet 43     Sonnet 44     Sonnet 45
Sonnet 46     Sonnet 47     Sonnet 48     Sonnet 49     Sonnet 50
Sonnet 51     Sonnet 52     Sonnet 53     Sonnet 54     Sonnet 55
Sonnet 56     Sonnet 57     Sonnet 58     Sonnet 59     Sonnet 60
Sonnet 61     Sonnet 62     Sonnet 63     Sonnet 64     Sonnet 65
Sonnet 66     Sonnet 67     Sonnet 68     Sonnet 69     Sonnet 70
Sonnet 71     Sonnet 72     Sonnet 73     Sonnet 74     Sonnet 75
Sonnet 76     Sonnet 77     Sonnet 78     Sonnet 79     Sonnet 80
Sonnet 81     Sonnet 82     Sonnet 83     Sonnet 84     Sonnet 85
Sonnet 86     Sonnet 87     Sonnet 88     Sonnet 89     Sonnet 90
Sonnet 91     Sonnet 92     Sonnet 93     Sonnet 94     Sonnet 95
Sonnet 96     Sonnet 97     Sonnet 98     Sonnet 99     Sonnet 100
Sonnet 101    Sonnet 102    Sonnet 103    Sonnet 104    Sonnet 105
Sonnet 106    Sonnet 107    Sonnet 108    Sonnet 109    Sonnet 110
Sonnet 111    Sonnet 112    Sonnet 113    Sonnet 114    Sonnet 115
Sonnet 116    Sonnet 117    Sonnet 118    Sonnet 119    Sonnet 120
Sonnet 121    Sonnet 122    Sonnet 123    Sonnet 124    Sonnet 125
Sonnet 126    Sonnet 127    Sonnet 128    Sonnet 129    Sonnet 130
Sonnet 131    Sonnet 132    Sonnet 133    Sonnet 134    Sonnet 135
Sonnet 136    Sonnet 137    Sonnet 138    Sonnet 139    Sonnet 140
Sonnet 141    Sonnet 142    Sonnet 143    Sonnet 144    Sonnet 145
Sonnet 146    Sonnet 147    Sonnet 148    Sonnet 149    Sonnet 150
Sonnet 151    Sonnet 152    Sonnet 153    Sonnet 154
```

```
_:$_="`'-.,_,.-'"x8;for(;;)
   {$y=substr$_,0,-1;print
      "$y\n";$_=(substr$_,-1).
         $y;sleep 0.9;}
            goto _; sleep
               (log the (flock_,_)). alarm_; do { it: _;

the: %vibrating ={ $phone, will, splice(@you), sideways =>};
   through   |plaster| to;   our %room;  where we    listen _,_;
for (;;){  the builder@s,  song;    autotuned to,   pop  }}
   until it  >>shift@s; $like=  b^a^t^t^l^e^me^n^ts   across ->
the, fancy,   split screen _;  kill (this);    pattern, dump
   it; along    the; map {as}   /c\/r\e\/n\u\/l\/a\/t\/i\/o\n/;
which: die@s,   in the winds   canonpath,           while
      i n t e r p o l a t i n g ;{   local alpine       hills };

far: %below=     _._.the.     crypt ~resonates,       ~over;
   an; $archaeological=     glob          (of)             ***mud;
pack (it), through;  %soundproof= pipe@s, all-the-way;  push@_;
```

```
$ perl dreaming_the_brown_note_up.pl
```

```c
int
main
(int _,char*
*__){char G[17][   77],
  x       ,    y,i,s,n,h;srand(time(0));    for
  (x=0;   x<77;x++)for(y=0;y<17;y++)G[y][x]=(rand()%100>   98?
'.':' ';memcpy(G[0]," ,-,",5);memcpy(G[1]," / ( ",5); memcpy(G[2],
" \\ ( ",5);memcpy(G[3]," `-`",5); n=rand()%15+ 10;for(i=0;i<n;i++){
s=(rand()%(77+17*2))-17*2;h=(rand()%(17-2))+1;for(x=0;x<h*2+1;x++){if
(s+x>=77){          family : on : a : trip          :continue;}
if(s+x<0){     ice : tumbles : down : the : mountain  :continue;}for
(y=0;y<h;y++){       in : clear : waterfall      :if(x-y==0){G[17-
1-y][s+x]='/';}else if(2*h-x-y==1){G[(17-1)-y][s+x]='\\';}else if(x-y
 >0&&2*h-x-y>0) G[(17-1)-y][s+x]=y>12-(rand()%5)?'*':rand()%30>
    y+22?'^':' ';}}}    for(y=0;y<17;y++){for(x=0;x<77;x
    ++)putchar(         G[y][x]);        putchar('\n')
                         ;}}
```

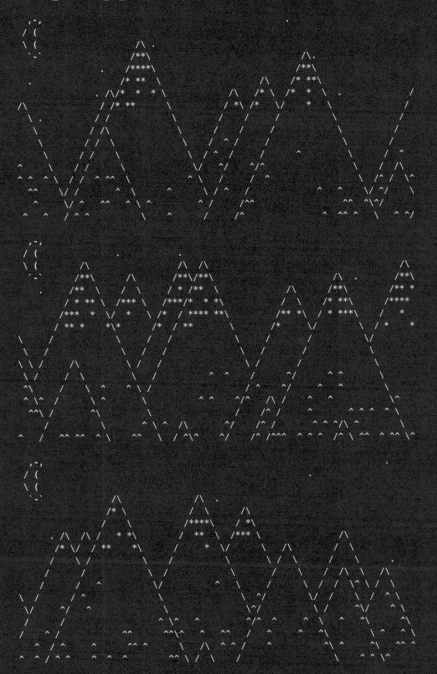

```haskell
import Data.List.Split;import System.Random;import Data.Char;
import Control.Concurrent;e=[-16..9];r=randomRIO(0,1);
d(j,k,a,b)[f,g,h]=max 0$min 7$9*((z$f+b-34-j)+(z$g-w-k))+h-a-35;
m o=v!!(minimum$map(d o)$chunksOf 3$map(fromIntegral.ord)p);
n=[(-5)..73];(&)=undefined;w=37;v="#*\"':,. ";z=abs;
main=(mapM_(\y->mapM(\x->do{a<-r;b<-r;return$m(mod x 32,z y,a,b)
})n>>=putStrLn)e>>threadDelay 1000000>>main);(#)=let{
```

```
_in the heian shrine            it echoed quietly = (&);
from above i watched        the carp under water = (&);
school children passed  looking right through me = (&);
i_ guiltily longed          to understand japanese = (&);


down the kamo river         side streets were full = (&);
restaurant balconies        hanging over the edge = (&);
i thought desperately          you would love this = (&);
reflected _in _the water    lights in_ the_ trees = (&);
```

```haskell
}in(&);p="+3).3(23)'2)*2).2&/2$62%92),1)/1&01$31)61(91);1)\
\$0)'0))0).0)00$10'60':0)<0)@0)(/),/)0/%4/#5/$6/'?/)%.)*.)\
\0.'1.#2.(3.#4.$5.'9.(;.%<.%=.'>.&&-(--)0-'1-#2-#3-%4-'7-#\
\8-%9-%:-&<-)$,)',&)$*,(/,(0,'1,$2,#3,&4,(5,#6,%8,&;,(>,)\
\(+)*+&++$,+$-+(.+(/+(0+'1+(2+#3+#4+%5+&9+(:+%<+)%*)**(+*$\
\,*$-*$/*(0*'1*#2*$3*&6*(7*$8*%9*&=*)))&.)&/)#0)#1)$2)$3)#\
\4)#5)%6)&9))*()/($0($1(&2(&5()9(.''/'#0'$1''.&'/&#0&'1&&\
\#%)%%)'%))%)+%',%'-%$.%#/%'0%)2%)4%)6%)8%):%)<%)>%)@%)B%)";
```

```
$ ghc alone_in_kyoto.hs && ./alone_in_kyoto
```

```
#define submerge const char*_=0%239?" ":"\t;\t";O*=2654435761;int
#define _c0b8(...) int s,on,__VA_ARGS__;int main(int O, char**Q)

 _c0b8(o_,     _o08ocQ0cOb,          _ocQbo8oo,         _o08ocOb_
  ){ ;              { ;;;                ;;}               ;{
   ;;               ;{                  ; }               {;;}
   }   float   the;;  static things ;; for (;;){ us :;;
  ; ;   break; the;  ;; long grass  ;unsigned squall  ; }
 { } ; while (1){soft:;  submerge us;;   in: sleep (0) ;
   ; ;   printf   (_);   quietly :on  ;;   the; soil:; };
  {{ };            ; ; ;;               ;{ ;             }; {
  {  ;   shake: time (1) ;register   *_, the =clock(s );
   ;} ; volatile   *_,   winds      ; ; double wills ;{
     ;  char the    ,*   fire      ;; short companion,*_;}
   ; {  union    {}*_, together  ;; ; void *warms  ;}
  } ;;            ;{;              ;} ;              ;;
    ; ; if (1) wet :;    raise   (1); struct{}ure  ;; ;
  ; ;  free (0);for(;;){ newborn :; ;    daughter :; ;
 ;{ ;  extern al,  **    world   ,*re;const ructed  ;};
 ;  ; ; continue;on:;;    floods   :; ;   of: water :;};}
 ; ;{ ; ;         ;; { ;         ;} ;            } ; ; }
```

```
$ cc water.c && ./a.out
                    ;
                                                        ;
                            ;       ;
                                          ;
            ;                             ;

        ;;      ;
                ;       ;
                              ;
                              ;         ;           ;
                                          ;


        ;                                           ;
        ;
        ;



                        ;
                        ;



                        ;




                        ;
```

```
             submarine =: 4 : 0

i=.(0{y)*(1&o.((1{y)*(x*0.2)+(2{y)*(o.2)))+2*((3{y)-0.5)
l =.(0 {y) *(2 &o.( ( 1{y)* (x* 0.2) +(2 {y) *( o.2) ) )
((( ((+/ "2)i) %2)+ 1) %2 ); (( (( (+/"2) l) %2) +1) %2)
)

                    0 : 0

    :               .                   .
  ,       below the fair and storm weather      :
     wave base, undulations                    ,
  .   encased in polyethylene,         ,        .
  ,   stranded steel and jelly:         .
   tri-core alternating current       ;
   translating water's circular motion        ,
     into linear power.
  .   the phase shifted relay
        makes Virginia and Devon glow        ,
  ,   like home                            .
  :         or a 60 foot pyrosome   ,           :
  . somewhere inbetween,                   .
        whose nub sieve dissolves ,            ,
   scant oxygen down secant slope.
  :    at the ceiling, engineers let     ,
  ,  oscilloscope speech rope out       .      .
   from a roll in the ship's hull.      .       .
  ;       the anchor drops          ,       :
  ,          :    the call              .
)
msg =:                  3 : 0
          w =. ? (4 4 3 $ 0)
          for_m. i.500 do.
o=.<.(((67*(>(0{(m submarine w))))<.67)
d =. <. (( 5* (>(1{(m submarine w))))<. 5)
s=.(<"1(|:(2 3$(i.3),d)))}(3 5$'-/|\-~}I{~=<:>=')
        (s o}(68#' '))1!:2[2
               (6!:3)0.01
                     end.

)
exit(msg'')
```

```
@echo off & setlocal enabledelayedexpansion
call :baro trauma      & call    :baro meter
call  :baro graph       & call    :baro grams
call    :baro que       & call   :alert
:baro
set /A              wind=%RANDOM% %%50
set /A           azimuth=%RANDOM% %%50
set        %~1=%wind% %azimuth% & exit /B 0
:approaching
if            %~2 GTR %~3 set %~1=%~3
if            %~2 LEQ %~3 set %~1=%~2
exit                   /B 0
:alert
for    /L %%B in (0,1,35) do (
set    "dead=" & set  "Lung=0 [o] ;  :  .       "
for    /L %%V in (0,1,50) do (
set     /A vein=%%V+!RANDOM! %%2
call    :ventilate fluid     !vein! %%B %trauma%
call   :ventilate sucks      !vein! %%B %meter%
call    :ventilate live       !vein! %%B %graph%
call   :ventilate pressure   !vein! %%B %grams%
call   :ventilate wall        !vein! %%B %que%
call   :approaching minimums   !fluid! !sucks!
call   :approaching minimums    !minimums! !live!
call   :approaching minimums     !minimums! !pressure!
call   :approaching minimums     !minimums! !wall!
if        !minimums! GTR 13   (set "dead=!dead! ") else (
call set                      labour=%%lung:~!minimums!,1%%
set                           dead=!dead!!labour!))
                              echo !dead!)
rem hibernate save energy wind down barotrauma nightmare
endlocal
:ventilate
set /A %~1=((30*(%~2-%~4)*(%~2-%~4)+(%~3-%~5)*(%~3-%~5)))/30
exit /B 0
```

```
;;o[o                              ;
 [[                             ::; ::
 [  [                  .              ]]
:] 0]:                               ]
:]00 ::                  :        .]]]]
 : 00]::              .: :.      o[[;;
 : 00]::                         ;;[[o
 : 00 ::               ;;        [[              ..
:]0  :                ::;;       [ [            :
  : 0]]:              ]]       ] 0 ::
]]  :                 ]]       ] 0 ::         .. :
]   ]]:              ]o ..     ] 00]]
 :   ]:              o[o;      : 0 ]:            ;;
:]0  :              ;;[o;    :] 0]]:         :: ;::
 [                   [ [      ] 0  ]:
 [[[[                [       ::]0  ]:           ]]
;;o[o;              :: 0  :   ] 0 ]          ..]o]]..
;;[[;               ] 0 ::   ] 00]:           ;oo;
 ]o  .              ::]0 ]:  :]]0 ]:         ;o[oo
 ]                  ]  ]]    :] 00 ]           [[
 ]                  ::  ]]:    [                [[
;  ;                ] 0 ]:     [[             :]00 ]:
 ;                  :]   ::    ;ooo            ]] ]]:
                    :]]00]::   oooo           ::]0 :
.. ::.              ::] 0 ]:  .. ]o .          : 0 ::
 :                  : 0 ::     ]]             :] 0 ]
                    :]]00]::                  :]00 ::
 .                   [        :; ::           :]] ]:
                    [ [        ;              :]   :
                   ;ooo;;                     :: 0 ]::
                    o[oo;    .. :             ] 0 ::
                    . oo                      :]  ]:
                     ]                         [
```

sensations =->{ start up on the ward;
tinting a};module Purple; flies=-> try{
to; redo; the operation every minute
encoding a surgeons shifting hand flutter
but the construct comes off false
letting the mind; return to formication}
                    end

```
c,q,g,p=1.45,0.5,
0.25,0.25;v=->x,t,s{
a,j=(x-c).abs,(t-q).abs
return j>p||a>2*g ? 0: (s*
-(2*p*g-p*a-g*j)).to_i+s;};(
1..1000).map{|m|;s="\n    " ; (
0..21).map{|t|;(0..74). map{
|x|;d=v[x/25.0,t/21.0, m];
s+=' .:-=+*&#%@'[d%11]};
s+="\n    "};sleep(0.02
);puts(s);'.:-=+*&'}
```

foul =->{ language scores nil; by mouth;
by day; mucous membranes line sheets
while legs do flick montaging decay
insects crawl together a wingless self;
for their entertainment in persistence do
make the patient lips plastically; yield
                        end end}

```
:..........        .........:
:..........        .........:
........ .            . .......
.......              .......
.....        @@        .....
.....       @@@@       .....
.....      @@@@@@      .....
.....      @@@@@@      ....
.....       @@@@       .....
........     @@       .......
.........            .........
:..........        .........:
:..........        .........:


@@°%%####&**+++**&&####%%@
@°####&&**++=++**&&####%%
%°####&&**++====++*&&####%
####&&**++==--==++**&&###
###&&**++=--;--==++**&&##
###&&**++=--:--==++**&&##
####&&**++==--==++**&&###
%°####&&**++====++*&&####%
@°°####&&**+++=++**&&####%%
@@°%%####&**+++**&&####%%@


::.  @@@°##&*+**&#°%%@@    .:
..  @@@°#&&*+=++*&#°%%@@
.  @@@°#&**+=-=++*&##°@@@
  @@°%#&**+=---=+*&&#°@@@
@@°##&*++=-:::-==+*&&#°@@@
@@°##&*++=-:::-==+*&&#°@@@
  @@°%#&**+=---==+*&&#°@@@
.  @@@°#&**+=-=++*&##°@@@
..  @@@°#&&*+=++*&#°%%@@   .
::.  @@@°##&*+**&#°%%@@   .:


%&+-:.@#&+-.:=*&%  :-=*#@
#&+-:.@#*=-.@ :=+&%  .:=*#
*+-:  %#*=:.@#%  .-+&%@.:=+
=::  %&*=:  %#*&%@.-+*#@.:-
:.  %&+-:  %&*=+*#@.-=*#@  :
:.  %&+-:  %&*=+*#@.-=*#@  :
=::  %&*=:  %#*&%@.-+*#@.:-
*+-:  %#*=:.@#%  .-+&%@.:=+
#&+-:.@#*=-.@ :=+&%  .:=*#
%&+-:.@#&+-.:=*&%  :-=*#@


.%*- #*- #+:@.=&@.=&%.=&@
#+:@#+:@&+:@&#  -*%.=&%.=&
+:@#+:@&=.%*-+#  -+#  -*#  -
.%&=.%*- %*-  .=&@:+#  -*#
%&=.%*- #+:@&%.=&%.=&@:+#
%&=.%*- #+:@&%.=&%.=&@:+#
.%&=.%*- %*-  .=&@:+#  -*#
+:@#+:@&=.%*-+#  -+#  -*#  -
#+:@#+:@&+:@&#  -*%.=&%.=&
.%*- #*- #+:@.=&@.=&%.=&@
```

```objc
/*go to the ant thou sluggard consider her ways and be wi*/
#import/*ants ar*/<Foundation/Foundation.h>/*y prepare th*/
/*eir me*/enum/*e s*/{W=79,/*o the an*/H=23};/*r of work */
/*give thought to her ways and be wise the ants are a peo*/
/*pl*/int main/* but t*/(int _,/*a store*/char* __[]) {/**/
/**/char M[W][H];/*ant you lazy p*/memset(M,' ',W*H);/* a*/
/*nd grow wise ants as creatures arent strong but they st*/
NSInteger xi,yi,/*ood in */x=45,y=15,d=0,i=0;/*nt you laz*/
while/*s conside*/(x>=0&&x<W&&y/* wise the ants*/>=0&&y<H){
/*not strong yet they store up their food in the summer g*/
BOOL t=/*e ant you slacke*/M[x][y]=='.'?/*s an*/NO:YES;/**/
/**/M[x][y]=M[x][y]==/*not strong yet t*/'.'?'o':'.';/*r */
/*food in the summer go to the ant thou sluggard consider*/
/*her */d=(4+d+/* wise the ants*/(t?1:-1))%4;switch(d){/**/
/*et they provide their food in the summer go to the ant */
case 0:y--;break;/*er*/case 1:x--;break;/* ants they are */
/*weak*/case 2:y++;/**/break;/*food in */case 3:x++;break;}
/*ople should learn a lesson from the way the ants live a*/
/*nts*/for(yi=0;yi<H;yi++)/*es y*/{for(xi=0;xi<W;xi++){/**/
/*in summe*/putchar(xi==x/*t you lazy*/&&yi==y?'@':/*ays */
/*and become wi*/M[xi][yi]);}putchar('\n');}/*ople yet th*/
/*ey provide their food in the summer go to the ant you s*/
/*luggard*/[NSThread sleepForTimeInterval:0.01];/*re a pe*/
/*opl*/i++;}return 0;}/*ey prepare their food in the summ*/
/*er go to the ant thou sluggard consider her ways and be*/
```

```
$ gcc Ants.m `gnustep-config --objc-flags` `gnustep-config --base-libs` && ./a.out

                              ..
                            .oo.
                            .ooo.
                             @..
                             ..



                           ..
                         ..o
                       .o..o.       ..
                      .oo.oo    .oo.
                      .o.o.ooooo...
                       ..oo.o....o.
                      @.ooo.oooo
                      o...o.o..o
                      o.ooo..oo.
                      ....oo.oo.
                       ooooo..oo
                     .o....ooooo.
                     ...ooooo..o.
                     .oo.   o..
                      ..      ..



                      ...........o@
                  ..   ...ooooo..oo.    ..
                 ..o .o.oooooo..ooo   .oo.
                .o..o.oo..oooooooo.ooooo...
                .ooo.o.o..o..ooo..oooo..o.
                .oooo..oo..oo.o..o.o.ooo
                .oooooooooo..oo..o.ooo..
                .ooooooo..o.o..oooo..  ..
               .oo..o.oo.oo.oo..oo.o....o.
                .ooooooooooo.o...oo.ooo....
                .oo..o..oooo....o..oo.....
               .oooo.o..oooooo..o..ooooo.
               .oooo...oo..oo..oo.o....
               .ooo.oo.oo.oooo.ooo..o...
               .oo..o.o..oo.o..oo..o...
                .oo.o.oo.oooooo....o.o.
                 ...o.o..ooo..o.....ooo.
                 .ooooooo.oooo.......o.
                 .oo.oo .. .oooooo.oo..
                 ....oo..   ...ooo.oo.o.
                 ...o..o.    .oo. ....
                  .oooo.        ..    ..
                   ....
```

```go
/*at the Olympic opening ceremony in Seoul*/
/*, a flock of doves flew into the big*/
/*cauldron. their wings melted to orange*/
/*like rings interlocked with rings.*/
/*they're betting all over the world*/
/*on when the cloud chamber will win*/
/*the lottery, free from faint astrology.*/
/*celestial bodies roll around the heavens*/
/*with the confirmation bias of a bowl.*/
/*you dream about the way the wind blew*/
/*that day as you turn over in your sleep*/


package main;
import(."time";."math";."math/rand";
."fmt");func main(){S,W,H,s:=[10][4]float64{},
39.0,12.0,0.05;Seed(Now().UTC().
UnixNano());for i:=range S{
S[i]=[4]float64{Float64()-0.5,
Float64()-0.5,Float64()-0.5,Float64()-0.5}};
for{for i,si:=range S{S[i][0]+=s*si[2];
S[i][1]+=s*si[3];for _,sj:=range S{
S[i][2]+=s*0.1*(sj[0]-si[0])+s*0.01*-si[0];
S[i][3]+=s*0.1*(sj[1]-si[1])+s*0.01*-si[1]}};
for y:=-H;y<H;y++{s:="";for x:=-W;x<W;x++{
n:=5;for _,b:=range S{f,g:=b[0]*W-x,b[1]*H-y;
d:=int(2*Sqrt(f*f+g*g));
if d<n{n=d}};s+="@ao:- "[n:n+1];
};Println(s);}; Sleep(50000000);}}
```

```
$ go run flocking.go
                          -::-                    -oao:
                          :oao-                   -o@a:
                          :a@o-        --         :o:-
                          -oo:       :oo-          --
                          --      --o@a:              --
                                  :oo:ao:            :o:-
                                 -o@a:::            -o@a:
                                  :a@o- :::-:-      -oao:
                                  :oao--oaooao-     -::-
                                  -:::- -o@oo@a:
                     ---          :aa-  -:o::o:-
                    :oo:          :aao-    - ---
                    :a@o-         :oo:
                    :oo:          --
                    ---


                                -::-
                                :aa:
                                :aa:
                                -- -::-
                                 :oo:                      -::-
                                 -o@a:                    -:aao-
                    :::          :ao:   :::- ::-          :ooao-
                   -oao--:-  -::- -oaa:-oao-     -o@a:o:
                   -o@o-oao-      -oaa::a@o-     -oao:-
                   -:o::a@o-       :o:--:o:-      -::-
                   - -oo:-              -   ---   :::-
                    ---                             -oao:
                                 -::-               -o@a:
                                 :aa:               :o:-
                                 :aao-              -
                                 -oo:
                                 --


                                    -                ---
                                 -:o:-             -oo:-
                                 -o@o:             :a@o-
                    -::-         -oao-             -oa:- -:-
                   :aao-           -   :::          -::--:ao:
                   :aao-  :o:-            --       :aa:-o@a:
                   -:o:    -o@o-           -oo:    :aa:oooo-
                    --     -oao-           :a@o- -::o@a:-
                            :::-           :aao- -:-:oo:
                                          -::- -oao-:-
                                                :a@o-
                                                -ooo-
                                                ---


                                 -::-
                                 :oao-
                                 :a@o-
                                 -:o:
                                 --
```

39

```
                    float
            /*Billie Jean*/ king = 1;
        float /*backhand in*/ tennis = 0.0;
         /*a*/void/*the net, one*/setup()
        {/*grip*/size(280,280);frameRate(40);
      push()/*ball*/;}/*a*/void draw/*ing King*/
    (){background(255); fill/*seats*/(220,253,80);
    circle(140,140,220); color Seles = color(255);
    set(5,0,Seles);point(40,15);/*rain*/ delay(1);
    float sinnet = 0.08 + (sin(king) + tan(king));
    king += /*6*/0.02; tennis += sinnet; noStroke();
    String gauge = "1.05 mm"; final float set = 6.0;
   String[] tension = match(gauge," "); double fault;
   pushStyle();fill(255);/*p*/int service = second();
  /*service*/box(0);saveStrings("4set3.txt",tension);
    strokeWeight(1); float net = tennis; long b0ll;
      for/*ty love*/(int/*o net*/ ball/*boy*/ = 0;
       ball <= width; ball/*boy please!*/ += 6)
      {float abuse /*wide*/ = /*se*/map/*hore*/
       /*++++++++++++++ SELES ++++++++++++++
            +++++++++++++ V +++++++++++++
             +++++++++ KEREK +++++++*/
              (sin(net),//,(ten)nis)
              -1.5, 1.5, 0, height);
              /*Snauwaert*/ellipse
                (ball,abuse,15,15);
              net+=/*6*/0.06/*6*/;}
               char racket = 'W';
                switch(racket)
                  {case 'W':
                   println
                   ("base");
                   break;
                   case 'L':
                   println
                   ("side");
                   break;
                   default:
                   /*Kerek*/
                   println
                   ("centre");
                   break
                   /*racket*/;}}
```

```
3♦Q♦Q♥A♦9♥9♥7♥3♥8♦Q♥9·9♥9♥8♥3♥5·Q♥9♥9♥9♥8♥3♥5·Q♥2·2 A♦A·A♥#  ♥J♠4♠
A♦A Q♥2♥3 Q♥5·2♥J·4 8♥J·4 8♥J·4 8♥J·5 # raised her heartless
2·2 A♦A·4 4♥Q♥2·2 A♦A·A 2 A♥Q♥9·3♦8♥A·2♦J·5 8♥7♦J·5 4♦3♦5♥J·#
5·4♥5♥J·5·4♥5♥J·9 5·8♦9♦J·9 4·8♥J·5 6♦7♦3♥J·9 2·# could be a real diamond
2·2 A♦A·4 4♥Q♥2·2 A♦A·A 2 A♥Q♥5·4♥3♦5♥A·2♦J·5 6♦7♦3♥J·4 8♥J·#♠8♥J♠4♠8
4 8♥J·4 8♥J·4 8♥J·4 8♥J·5 2♥J·4 8♥J·4 8♥J·4 8♥J·4 8♥J·#♠5♣
5·8♥3♥J·9 4·8♥J·5 8♥3♦Q♥2·2 A♦A·4 4♥Q♥2·2 A♦A·A 2 A♥#
9·8♥5♦A 2♦J·9 8♥5♦J·5 4♥5♥9♦J·5 4♥5♥9♦J·9 9♥8·# let's chance the next line
2·2 A♦A·4 4♥Q♥2·2 A♦A·A 2 A♥Q♥5·4♥5♥A·2♦J·9 5·8♦9♦J·9 8♥6♦J·#
9·2♦Q♥2·2 A♦A·4 4♥Q♥2·2 A♦A·A 2 A♥Q♥9·8♥5♦A 2♦J·9 8♥5♦J·#♥5♥
5·6♥7♦3♥J·9 3·8♥J·4 8♥J·4 8♥J·4 8♥J·5 2♥J·4 8♥J·4 8♥J·#
9·3♦8♥J·5 8♥7♦J·5 4♥5♥9♦J·5 4♥9♦Q♥2·2 A♦A·4 4♥# that was her typeface
2·2 A♦A·A 2 A♥Q♥5·4♥5♥9♦A 2♦J·5 4♥5♥9♦J·5 4♥5♥9♦J·9 5·8♦9♦J·#
5·4♥5♥J·9 4·8♥J·5 4♥3♦5♥J·5 8♥7♦J·5 4♥3♦5♥J·5 4♥5♥9♦J·# shuffle on a bit
5·4♥3♦5♥J·4 8♥J·4 8♥J·4 8♥J·5 2♥J·4 8♥J·4 8♥J·4 8♥J·5 8♥7♦J·#
5·8♥7♦J·5 9♥J·4 8♥J·9 3♦8♥J·9 3♦8♥J·4 8♥J·4 8♥J·4 8♥J·#♣4♥Q
4 8♥J·9 5·8♦9♦J·9 8♥5♦J·9 9♥7♦9♦Q♥2·2 A♦A·4 4♥#    never could concentrate
2·2 A♦A·A 2 A♥Q♥5·4♥5♥A·2♦J·4 8♥J·4 8♥J·4 8♥J·5 2♥J·4 8♥J·#8♥J♠7♠
4 8♥J·4 8♥J·5 8♥7♦J·5 8♥6♦J·6 8♥5♦Q♥2·2 A♦A·4 4♥# should've packed more
2·2 A♦A·A 2 A♥Q♥5·8♥6♦A 2♦J·5 8♥6♦J·5 9♥J·5 9♥J·4 8♥J·5 9♥J·#
5·8♥7♦Q♥2·2 A♦A·4 4♥Q♥2·2 A♦A·A 2 A♥Q♥5·9♥A·2♦J·9 3·8♥J·#♥6♦J♠4♠8
9·3♦8♥J·7 9♥4♦Q♥2·2 A♦A·4 4♥Q♥2·2 A♦A·A 2 A♥Q♥7 8♥2·A 2♦J·#
8·8♥9♦Q♥2·2 A♦A·4 4♥Q♥2·2 A♦A·A 2 A♥Q♥5·4♥5♥9♦A 2♦J·# sorry typing face
5·4♥3♦5♥J·4 8♥J·4 8♥J·4 8♥J·5 2♥J·4 8♥J·9 3·8♥J·#2♠A♠A♠A♠
5·4♥3♦5♥J·4 8♥J·5 9♥J·5 9♥J·9 3·8♥J·5 4♦9♦Q♥2·2 A♦A 4 4♥#
2·2 A♦A·A 2 A♥Q♥5·9♥A·2♦J·4 8♥J·9 3·8♥J·9 3·8♥J·5 8♥6♦J·#♦Q♥2♠2
4 8♥J·9 3·8♥J·5 8♥3♦J·5 8♥6♦J·4 8♥J·4 8♥J·4 8♥J·5 2♥J·4 8♥J·#
4 8♥J·4 8♥J·7 8♥2·J·5 9·3♦8♥J·5 8♥6♦J·4 8♥J·9 2·# staring at the papers
2·2 A♦A·4 4♥Q♥2·2 A♦A·A 2 A♥Q♥5·8♥6♦A 2♦J·5 4♥3♦5♥J·#
5·4♥3♦4♥9♦Q♥2·2 A♦A·4 4♥Q♥2·2 A♦A·A 2 A♥Q♥5·9♥A·2♦J·5 8♥6♦J·#8♥J♠4♠
4 8♥J·4 8♥J·4 8♥J·5 8♥6♦J·7 8♥2·J·4 8♥J·4 8♥J·4 8♥J·4 8♥J·#♠8♥J♠
5·2♥J·4 8♥J·4 8♥J·4 8♥J·4 8♥J·4 8♥J·5 8♥7♦J·9 3·8♥J·5 6♦7♦#
2·2 A♦A·4 4♥Q♥2·2 A♦A·A 2 A♥Q♥5·9♥A·2♦J·5 8♥7♦J·5 4♥5♥9♦#♥J♠5♠
2·2 A♦A·4 4♥Q♥2·2 A♦A·A 2 A♥Q♥5·9♥A·2♦J·7 8♥5♦# what will it say for Cancer
2·2 A♦A·4 4♥Q♥2·2 A♦A·A 2 A♥Q♥5·8♥6♦A 2♦J·5 8♥6♦J·4 8♥J·#8♥J♠4
4 8♥J·7 8♥2·J·5 6♥7♦3♥J·4 8♥J·4 8♥J·4 8♥J·4 8♥J·5 2♥J·4 8♥J·#
4 8♥J·4 8♥J·4 8♥J·4 8♥J·5 5♥6♦Q♥2·2 A♦A·4 4♥#    why would I have a spade
2·2 A♦A·A 2 A♥Q♥5·8♥7♦A 2♦J·5 4♥5♥J·5 8♥7♦J·9 3·8♥J·9 3·8♥J♠
4 8♥J·4 8♥J·7 8♥2·J·5 4♥3♦5♥J·5 6♥7♦3♥J·5 4♥5♥J·9 5·8♦9♦J·#4♥Q♥
5·8♥3♥J·5 8♥6♦J·4 8♥J·5 2♥J·7 8♥2·J·5 6♥7♦3♥J·# clubbing could be seals
5·4♥5♥9♦2·2 A♦A·4 4♥Q♥2·2 A♦A·A 2 A♥Q♥9·5·8♦9♦A 2♦J·5 4♥5♥9♦J·#
9·8♥6♦J·9 8♥6♦J·9 5·8♦9♦J·5 4♥5♥9♦J·5 4♥5♥9♦J·5 4♥5♥J·#2♠A♥Q
5·4♥5♥9♦J·5 4♥5♥9♦J·5 4♥3♦5♥J·5 9♥J·5 4♥3♦5♥J·9 8♥5♦J·# it suits
9·8♥5♦J·9 8♥6♦J·9 8♥5♦J·5 4♥5♥9♦J·5 2♥J·9 9♥9♥9♥2♥Q A 3 2·K♦K♦#5♠6♥7♠
```

42

```
$ ante blinds.ante

       b/sddyhoso
      +hOMmeyNMMo`
      `/mmmmydhs/sms
      //-``       yMd
      /...-- --``:os
      `s -- - ``. `+.
      :`. .s/.   .:
        /`///1.  :o
        /d/``  :sody+.
    :o9mNNymmdmms-sMMNMm


       `/sddyhovo
      +hNMmmeyNPMo`
      `/mpmmydhs/sms
      //-``       yMe
      /.1.-- -0``<os
      `s --`0 ``. `+.
      :`. 1s0.    .:
        /`-//0.  :o
        0d/``  :sody+.
    :o:mNNymmdmms-sMMNMm


       c/sddyhovo
      +hPMmmeyNPMo`
      `/mmmmydhs/sms
      //-``       yMf
      /...-- -0``:ns
      `s -- - ``. `+.
      :`. 1s0.    .:
        /`-/-..  :o
        /d/``  :sody+.
    :o8mNNymmdmms-sMMNMm


       c/sddyhovo
      +hNMmmdyNPMo`
      `/mnmmydhs/sms
      //-``       yMe
      /./.-- -0``=os
      `s --`. ``. `+.
      :`. 1s/.    .:
        /`//-0.  :o
        0d/``  :sody+.
    :o9mNNymmdmms-sMMNMm


       c/sddyhouo
      +hOMmmfyNOMo`
      `/mmmmydhs/sms
      //-``       yMf
      /.0.-- -.``:ns
      `s --`- ``. `+.
      :`. 0s..    .:
        /`//-1.  :o
        /d/``  :sody+.
    :o9mNNymmdmms-sMMNMm
```

```
v                    >"___",,,v
>        "_",55*:>|    down1town's writer's block
                 :$ freezes-the souk in
             ^              <
     v ,*52,"_"< place though can't decide
     3    if it's a >1-          v bazaar
     7 >v           ^,,,<  <       #
     * ^#       or an > ^ < ancient city
     >:|:    <  planned "    >  v by alien jokers
      $#          # _   >^>" $ "v
      "so moVe through _  >???" @ "v white
  v<< |      #      `#> > ^>v>" # "v
  ,"" "    space >    ^ " ^    <    < aVoiding black crystal
  ,__ ,#     #   ^"_|_"???"_| "^
  ,_| 5graphemes^" |_"???" |  "^ expertly stroked in
  1__ 5      #    ^   <"^"> # ^#
  -"" *   neVer hands _   brushing corners
  :^?<:#    #  out on _ _        the run
   ^ _$"|",@            _ _
      :     #          " "
  >   ^               ^< >^
      >        "|",55*:|:   <  <
                       $
              ^-1,*52,"|"<
```

44

```
using System;using System.Threading;class _{object

/*.1.Ealing Broadway......................1.min..*/
watching, the, clock, like, a, sex_worker,
soon, to, be, badly, reviewed, online;
ulong for_getting(){up: while(0==0){
the: exam: _is: still: going:
or: of: filling: every: blank: with:
the_: space: between: double seconds;}}

/*.2.West Ruislip.........................3.mins.*/
static void Main(){object the,_=0, carriage;
Random end=new Random();

/*.3.Ealing Broadway......................6.mins.*/
_the: gap:  between: Liverpool: Street: and: Bank:
where: you: wonder: if (0==0){
there: _is: enough: blood: in_: the: bodies:
on: the_: whole: central: line:
to: fill: St:Pauls: cathedral: _=_;}

/*.4.Hainault.............................8.mins.*/
string thoughts = System. IO.  File.  ReadAllText(
"clock_in_clock_out.cs"). Replace("\n",""),

/*.5.White City..........................12.mins.*/
what, small, section, of, _the, tunnel,
would, it, flood,
your,  mind,  rocking, towards,  _the_, red, line,
of_, the_, second, hand,
its, vein;

/*.6.Hainault............................17.mins.*/
while(0==0){Console.Write(thoughts. Substring(end.
Next(0,thoughts. Length - 30), end.Next(15,30)));
Thread.Sleep(25);}}}
```

```
$ mcs clock_in_clock_out.cs && ./clock_in_clock_out
```

/*.Calling at:.nd, hand,its, vCalling at:................. bodies:on: the_: who
le: cent5.Edgware...................Street: and: Ban(end.Next(0,tho...........
...*/watching, t_the: gap: betwee1.Edgware.................. in_: the: bodies:
on: tecond, hand,its, vein;/*.6.KedAllText("clockeadAllText("clock_in_clockflood
,your, mind, sex_worker,soon, to,watching, the, clock, likennel,would, it, floo
d,yo.High.Barnet..........: whole: central: line:to...............*/static void
gh: blood: in_: the: bo: double seconds;}}/*.2.ne:to: fill: St:Pauls fill: St:Pa
uls:section, of, _t*/while(0==0){Con/*.Calling at:.filling: every: blank: with:a
ndom();/*.3.High.Barnet.................3.mins.*/etting(){up: while(0=cond, han
d,its, Threading;class _ank: with:the_: spacebodies:on: the_: whole: cent("clock
_in_clock_out...8.mins.*//*.Calling ....1...............1ank:_in: w
hich: youhe: exam: _is: still: goi: the: bodies:onhe: gap: between: Liverpoolou
gh: blood: in_: the: bod.....*/_the: gap: betetting(){up: while(0==0){th.......
............*/_ tunnel,would, i....12.mins.*//*.....................0){the: exam
: _i.........8.mins.*//*.Calling void Main(){object the.......8.mins.*//*.Callin
gNext(15,30)));Thread.Sleep(10g(){up: while(0==0)*.2.High.Barnetins.*//*.Calling
 at:...............17.mins.*//*.ring thoughts = eadAllText("clock_in_ctem.Thread
ing;cCalling at:..*/what:
central: line:to: fil......................................*/watching, the tu
nnel,would, it, flood,yo.............*/static v...............................
.........*/static vill: St:Pauls: cathed...................ng: every: blank: wit
h:the_: in_: the: bodies:on: t""),/*.5.Edgware...............................oo
n, to, be, badly, rlock_in_clock_out.cs")thoughts. Lengt*//*.Calling at:.......
.............................net................/while(0==0){Console.Wr
ite,would, it, flood,your, min.................12.m.12.mins.*//*.Calling at:..
.........*/static void line;ulong for_gettins.*//*.Calling at:..................
......1.min..*/...6.mins.*//*.Calli.Next(15,30)));Thread.S: blood: in_: the: btt
ing(){up: while(0==0){th _the, tunnel,would, it, ...*/watchi......
..............s: enough: blood: ine(0==0){Console.Write(thought......1.min..*//*
.Calling5.Edgware.................h - 30), end.Next(15,30, rocking, towardadly
, reviewed, om();/*.3.High.Barnet...................*/static vo St:Pauls: cath..
.................*/whdies:on: the_: whole: centrs.*//*.Calling at:..............
....*/sing, the, clock........*/_the:30), end.Next(15,30)));Threa end.Next(15,30
)));Thread.=0){there: _is: enough: blou: wonder: if (0==0oing:or: of: filling: e
...............6.mins...............12.mstill: going:or: of: filling:..........
...............6.mins.*//ed, online;ulong for_getting.......*/string thoughts =
Synnington........he_: space: between: ....e("\n",""),/*.5.
Edgware.......,soon, to, be, badly, reviace: between: doub exam: _is: still: goin
g......................1t.................od,your, mind, online;ulong for cloc
k, like, a, sexsling at:............................8.mins.*...............
.....nington.....ins.*//*.Callinon................. line:to: fill:onds;}}/*
.2.High.Barne.......17.mins.*//*.C...1.
min..*//*.C,would, it, flood,your, mi:or: of: filling: every: blf_, the_, secon
d, hand,its, ...*/watching, t flood,your, mind, rocki, end.Next(15,30)))
;Thread...................g, the, clock, like, a, sex0, carriage;Random end=ne
w R..................*/while(0==0){Co.12.mins.*//*.Calling at end.Next(15,30)));
Tnd.Next(0,thoughts...........3.mins.*//*.Call, of, _the, tunnens.*//*.Calling a
t:..ne,of_, the_, second, handystem. IO. File. ReadAlldom end=new Random();/*.
3.Hig - 30), end.Next(15,30)));Tith:the_: space:.....6.mins.*//*.Calling a(0,tho
ughts. Length - 30), ...6.mins.*//*alling at:..........sing System.Threading;cl
ass /*.1.Edgware................................... hand,its, vein;/*.6.Khoughts
. Substring(end.Nexis: still: goingNext(15,30)));Thread.Sleep(h.Barnet..........
...................8.mins exam: _is: still: goin;}/*.4.Mill Hill East........lon

47

```python
from random import random as r          #
from numpy  import zeros  as z #
                    #
the, fire='station' is 'getting', 'ready'
  #
w,h=77,19;s=z([h,w],str);b=z(w*h+w+1,int)
                #
to, hatch = all ('its'), 'trucks'   #
                    #
while 1:  #
                        #
 the= 'night' is 'daydreaming'
        #
 for _ in range(w//9):b[int((r()*w)+w*(h-1))]=40
            #
 of, a, blaze = 'so', 'big',()
        #
 for i in range(w*h):  #
  b[i]=(b[i]+b[i+1]+b[i+w]+b[i+w+1])//4
  if i<w*h-1:s[i//w,i%w]=" .:^*xsS#$"[min(b[i],9)]
                        #
 management = 'will' + 'attend'
                    #
 print('\n'.join(''.join(l) for l in s))
            #
'' in their, little — van #
```

```
$ python firefighting.py


                                        .
    ...                                 .                              .:.
   .:.. ...:..                         .....                         .*x*:.
   .......:^*^::.                     .::::::. ...              ..    :xsx*^.
     .....^*xx*:.              ..    .:^^^^^^::^^^::::.     ..::.   .*xxx*:
     .....:*xx*^.          ...::::....:^*******xsx*xxx*:    .^^^:    .:**x*:
    .::....:^**:.        .::::^^^^^^::^*xxxxxxsSSS###S*.   :^*^.   .:^**x*:
  ..:^x*:. .:::.   .... .^*^^^^^^^*xssx*^*xxsssssS#$$$$#s^.  :**^:..:*xxxxxx*.
.:*^:*sx:   :^:   :^:...:*****xx**x###s**xsssssxsS######x:  .^***^^xS#Sssxss*
*S#S*^xx:  .xs^  :sS*..^xx^^^*ss*:*S$$S*^***xsx^^xx*xS$$$*..:^s$$SsS$#sSSxssS
$$$$#*ss:  .xS*  s$$*  ^#$*..:*x:.:xssSSS$$*:*^:.::.^#$$$*:xx^s$$$Sx#$S##*^^$
$$$$$$xx.   ^*:  s$$:  .#$x$$$..   .:.s$$$$x ..     .s#Sx::xx:^#$$s:S$Sss:  $
$$$$$$..         :x^    ^x:$$$        :xxSS:         .:..  ..  :*x: :x^..


                                                                    .:.
         .                                                          :^:.
        .::.                                    .::..               .:::.
        .::.                           .......:^^^^^:.              .:::.
        ....                    ..   .::::::^***xxx*:       .     ...:::.
  ...      .               .....::^:....:^^^^^^^*xxsssx^.    .......::::::::..::
:..::      .     .     ......:::::^**^:::^^^^^^^^**xxxxx^.   .::^:::^**^^^^^^^*xs
x*^^:.    ..   .::.   :::::::::..:^***^***^::::::^^^xss*:. .:^*x***xx***^^*s#$$
$#x^:.   .....^**:  .:^^^*^:.. .:^^**xx*^:.     ..^xSs*:::::^xSSx*xxxx*^^x#$$$
$$#*^:.   .:^*ssx^. .^^**xx^.  :^^*^*xx*:.     .^x##S*:^x*^^*SSx^^*ssx**s$$$$
$$$x*s*.   :x#$#s*^:^**^*xs*: .^xx*^:^^:::::. .^s$$$$s*x$#*:*Ss*:.^*x*^*sSsx*
xS#xxSx.:x:.x$$S*xx*s$s..^xx^ .^xx^.  . :xSS#s^^S$$$$#*s$$$xsSSs^ .:::::^^*s^
.^*::*^$$$x $$S*:^^:S$s  .:^.  .::.$$ $$$xSS$$x.^$$$$x:^$$$Sxx$$$$$$    . x$x
       $$x: $$:     :x:            $$ $$$.::*x:  :**^.  ^SS^..$$$$$$      :x


                                                                   .
                                           ......                   .
                                          .:::^^^:.                 .
                                .    .......:^^****^:.              .    .....
                              .::. ..........::^^^^^.         ......::......:^***^
:..                           .:::.:::.     ..::^**:.     .:^^::^^:::::^*ssSSs
*^:.      ..::.    ...:.      .::::^^:.       .^*x*^:..  .^**^^^^^^^^^^^xS####
s*^:.     .^**^:. ...::^^.    :::::^^:.      .:xSSs*^:^^::^**^:::^*^::*xsSSSS
s*^^:.   .^xxx*:..:^:::^^:   .:^::..:...:....:*S$$#x**ssx^****:::^^:.:^*xxxxx
*^^^:^^:.:xSsx^^^^*x*:..::.  .:::^::^*^****^:^x#$$$s**S$Sxxsssx^^^:. .:^*xssx
*^:::*x*:^xSx**SSxxSs*:::*x:   .^sx*xSssSSx*^^x#$$S*:^s$#xs#$$$#s*. .^x*^*s$$
$S: .^*^.:*x^^#$$$#$$Ssx*#$*    *Ss*xSssSs^:.:s#x*xsx$$S*^x#$$$$s^. :S$x::^#$
$$.  ...  ...:S$$$$$$#sx^sS$$$  :*$$:^:^^:.  .x$$ x$$$$s..:***SS^$$ .sS$$  ^$
$^             :xsxxxx^:...:$$$    $$           .$$ :xxSS:     .:: $$  .:$$
```

```
exec('''from sys import stdout as i;from time import sleep
from random import choice as together,random as dream
from collections import defaultdict as into;deep=9999''')
```

```
"-!- pttr [~pttr@l3-4.members.linode.com] has joined #irc"

"<@pttr>  ";_=open('irc'). read(). split(' '); slice
"<@pttr>  "; distant, digital= locals, compile; pass
"<@pttr>  "; all('are'); set('free') and 'world', open
"<tstar>  ";'''in 'cold';__,minds= zip, into (list),
"<tstar>  ";[minds[signal].append(s) for signal,s in (all,
            __(__(_,_[            1:],_[2:]),_[3:]))[1]]


"<+wd1409>"; lambda laughter: complex (intoxication)
"<+wd1409>"; display =help, hex or reversed('pattern')
"<ulter>  "; us=together([shed for sorrow,shed in('heart',__(*[
"<ulter>  ",_,range(deep)][1:]))[1] if sorrow in 'part\n'[-1]])
"<ulter>  ";_,left=together,          (_[us],_[us+1],_[us+2])

while' ':
 "<murphy>"; afterward= minds, filter, hash, exit
 "<daeros>"; dead='#channel'; alone= left[0]=='\n'
 "<@pttr> "; i.write(('am i?',left[0]+' '*(1-alone))[1])
 "<@pttr> "; _;sleep(4*(alone+.1)*dream()); 'of', next;
 "<tstar> "; left=left[1],left[2],together(minds[left])


"-!- pttr [~pttr@l3-4.members.linode.com] has left #irc"
```

```
$ python irc.py

<@tarmon_herra> 20
<@tarmon_herra> <stretton-bs> Every time I come here, the number of people just
shrinks. :c
<stretton-bs> I love Superman.
<@kingkunta> -_-
<@kingkunta> How is life?
<otherguy101> ?
<otherguy101> Good
<otherguy101> I should've just kept them to myself
<otherguy101> and not some structure
<deadzow> You could be my man-servant
<deadzow> I don't think Wolf Blass do a zinfandel, therefore I don't drink beer
either
<@deathrow> Aye
<daeros> lol
<daeros> some dude was pretending to be you?
<daeros> sounds like he mad
<@tarmon_herra> Haven't et anything you've made which has been hard
<@stiffstyles> i.e you lose money
<@stiffstyles> only way to say MMORPG..
<@Sadis> anyway, dont kill yourself, cause this conversation would make  me look
 real bad
<Semilanceata> shit
<Semilanceata> oh hey crab77apple
<PAPASMURF> crab77apple
<PAPASMURF> crab77apple
<crab77apple> oh
<crab77apple> path isn't right
<crab77apple> I don't think Moose has made any spam posts
<@tarmon_herra> Try to wave a sock in front of the comp case
<@tarmon_herra> And at least it'll be a hot sunny 15C day when I'm riding over
<@deathrow> Don't think there's a niche to be exploited
<@stiffstyles> inflation will incrase
<crab77apple> lolicon - yeah, I couldn't find the checkers
<lolicon> so apparently i read somewhere
<lolicon> that was a weird sentence
<PAPASMURF> maybe someone else
<@tarmon_herra> How much closer?
<@deathrow> I'll try to grab a screeny soonish
<Mynameaborat> Top left of the crag is pretty indistinct though
<@medellin> and you just go buy food for your wife and shit
<@stiffstyles> at least japan
<lolicon> when i look at japanese writing
<@medellin> one or two fingers up eachother butt, for the connection
<@medellin> oops mispaste
<@medellin> the free mode vote thing
<@medellin> it is so, so bad
<@Sadis> cant find it anymore
<@medellin> would you be looking at the past of the satelites
<Semilanceata> since civilians take refuge in being the "weaker" side in a way t
eamkilling is makes 1vx very possible
<@Sadis> that looks cute
```

```erlang
-module(fourohfour). -export([for/0,for/1]). oh(Fo,Oh,_)when
Fo<Oh->Oh;oh(Fo,_,Oh) when Fo>Oh->Oh;oh(Fo,_,_)->Fo. for(Oh)
->Fo=30,Of=11,Fou=fun lists:nth/2,Ohf=fun lists:concat/1,Ou=
fun lists:seq/2, Our=fun round/1, Foo=fun math:cos/1,OhF=fun
math:sin/1,OhFor=fun io:format/2,ForO=fun timer:sleep/1,Fu=[
"                                                           ",
"      444444444       000000000        444444444           ",
"      4::::::::4      00:::::::::00     4::::::::4           ",
"      4:::::::::4    00:::::::::::::00  4:::::::::4          ",
"     4::::44::::4   0:::::::000:::::::0 4::::44::::4         ",
"    4::::4 4::::4   0::::::0   0::::::0 4::::4 4::::4        ",
"   4::::4  4::::4   0:::::0     0:::::0 4::::4  4::::4       ",
"  4::::4   4::::4   0:::::0     0:::::04::::4   4::::4       ",
" 4::::444444::::4440:::::0 000 0:::::04::::444444::::444     ",
" 4::::::::::::::::40:::::0 000 0:::::04::::::::::::::::4     ",
" 4444444444:::::4440:::::0     0:::::04444444444:::::444     ",
"          4::::4   0:::::0     0:::::0          4::::4       ",
"          4::::4   0:::::0     0:::::0          4::::4       ",
"          4::::4   0:::::::000:::::::0          4::::4       ",
"        44::::::44  00:::::::::::::00         44::::::44     ",
"        4::::::::4    00:::::::::00           4::::::::4     ",
"        4444444444     000000000             4444444444     ",
"                                                           "]
,Foh=Ohf([""                    ""++[Fou(oh(Our(Frr*Foo(Oh)-Off*OhF(Oh)
)+ Fo,1,57), Fou(oh(Our(Frr*OhF(Oh) +Off*Foo(Oh)) +Of,1,18),
Fu)) || Frr<-Ou(-Fo,Fo)]++"\n" || Off<-Ou(-Of,Of) ]), OhFor(
"~s" , [Foh] ), ForO( 50 ), for(Oh + 0.1). for()->for(0.0).
```

```
$ erlc fourohfour.erl && erl -noshell -s fourohfour for
```

```
   444444444        000000000              444444444
   4:::::::4       00:::::::::00            4:::::::4
   4:::::::4      00:::::::::::::00          4:::::::4
   4:::44:::4    0:::::::000:::::::0         4:::44:::4
   4:::4 4:::4   0::::::0   0::::::0         4:::4 4:::4
   4:::4  4:::4  0:::::0     0:::::0         4:::4  4:::4
   4:::4   4:::4 0:::::0     0:::::0         4:::4   4:::4
   4:::4    4:::44440::::0 000 0::::04:::4    4:::44:::4   :::444
   4:::::::::::::::::40::::0 000 0::::04:::::::::::::::::::4
   4444444444:::::4440::::0     0::::04444444444:::::444
         4:::4  0:::::0     0:::::0               4:::4
         4:::4  0:::::0     0:::::0               4:::4
         4:::4  0:::::::000:::::::0               4:::4
       44:::::44 00:::::::::::::::00           44:::::44
       4:::::::4  00:::::::::::00              4:::::::4
       4444444444   000000000                 4444444444


                         000000::00   44:::::4
                         0:::::::::::00   4:::4
                         00::::::::::::0   4:::4   4444444
                44444    00:::::0000:::::0   4:::::444:::::4
          44444:::4      0:::::0   00::::0444:::::::::4:::4
          4:::::::44      0:::::0    0::::04::::::44444:::4
          44:::::4        0:::::0    0::::0444:::4    4:::4
          4:::4           40::::0 000 0::::0  4:::4   4:::4
          4:::4    44444440::::0 000 0:::::0   4:::4 4:::4
          4:::::444::::::40::::0       0:::::0    4:::44:::4
        444::::::::44:::4 0:::::0      0:::::0    4:::::4
        4:::::::444 4:::4  0:::::0      :::::0     4:::::::
        444:::::4  4:::4  0:::::::000:::::0        4::444444
           4:::4  ::::4   0::::::::::::::00        444
           4:::4 4:::4    00:::::::::000
           4::44:::4        00000000
           4:::::::4
           4:::::::4


          444::4:::::4  000:0000
          44:::::4  0::::::::00
           ::::44  0::::::::::00
           4:::::440:::::::::::000
          44 4:::44:40::::::000::::0
          44:::::4 40:::::0   0::00
          44:::::4  0:::::0   0::::
           44:::4  0:::::0 0   :::::00
          44:44 0::::00 000 0:::::0
          44:4 0::::0   00 0:::::00
             44  0::::   0:::::0    44:44
                 0:::  0:::::00  44::::44
                 0:::00 00::::044::::::::::44
                 0::::::::::::004::::::::4:::::44
                 00::::::::::04::::::44  4:::::4
                  00::::::::0 44::44    4:::44
                  00:0::::0   44::44 4::::4
```

53

`'[}((({]){[[)]))[{]()}]()]{})()(]}'`

```
___,_=     {{Wake,up,  {late} and {{the, children},
            {are,  already},  {at,  {the,     park}}}},
         {{{Air, drifts},through, {the, curtains}}
            and {there, are, {{8, {hours}},ahead}},
            of, {{silence}   and      {childrens,
            laughter  }}  and {{  the,  thermals},
            _return,  {thoughts}, from, yesterday}}},{}


____=      [[=[Open]  them   [=on   [=the   [stack]=]=],
            [=indented   [=[deep]=]  in   [=long
            [symbolic] expressions=]   [Each node]
          [=[=a   [leaf]  =]   [=folding   [open]=]=],
            [revealing]  [=[  future     actions]
              so [in  winter]=]  [=[=you  [think]=]
            [=the [process]=]  will   [never  end]=]=]]


___=0>0     and  (today  (the.root)  (is.visible).
            which.means  (slowly   ((faithfully))).
            the  (stack  (starts   (to. collapse))).
            Branches  (wrapping. themselves) .in_
          ((parentheses)).  closing  and  faster(
            they.tumble)._until (it.is)-5-PM and
            the (children (have.left). the. park))
```

```
loadstring("__:gsub('.',function(v)table.insert(_,v)end)for k=1"..
",#_-1 do j=k for i=k+1,#_ do j=_[i]<_[j] and i or j end _[k],_".."
"[j]=_[j],_[k];print(unpack(_));os.execute('sleep 0.1');end")()
```

```
$ lua stack.lua

(    }    [    (    {    {    ]    )    {    [
[    ]    )    )    [    {    (    }    }    ]
[    )    ]    {    }    )    (    (    ]    }
(    (    (    }    {    {    ]    )    {    [
[    ]    )    )    [    {    [    }    }    ]
[    )    ]    )    (    (    (    (    ]    [
(    (    (    (    {    {    [    )    {    [
[    )    ]    )    (         }    (    ]    ]
(    )    (    )    (         )    )    {    (
[    ]    ]    )    [         [    }    }    ]
[    )    ]    {    }    )    }    {    {    ]
(    (    (    (    )    )    ]    {    {    [
[    ]    )    )    [    )    [    {    ]    [
[    )    ]    (    )    )    {    {    {    (
[    ]    ]    [         {    )         {    (
[    {    }    {    }    )    }         ]    }
(    (    (    (    (         )    )    )    )
[    ]    ]    )    [         {    ]    }    ]
[    {    ]    {    [         [    {    }    [
(    (    (    (    (         )    )    )    )
[    [    [    (    [    ]    {         }    [
{    (    ]    (    ]    }    {    ]    ]    ]
(    (    (    (    (    (    )    ]    (    {
(    {    }    }    }    ]    ]    {    ]    {
(    (    (    (    (    (    )    )    (    (
[    [    [    (    [    ]    ]    ]    ]    ]
{    {    }    }    }    ]    ]    {    {    {
(    (    (    (    (    )    )    )    )    )
[    [    [    (    [    ]    ]    {    ]    ]
(    (    (    (    (    (    )    )    )    )
[    [    [    (    [    ]    ]    ]    ]    ]
{    {    {    {    {    }    }    {    {    {
(    (    (    (    (    )    )    )    )    )
[    [    [    (    [    ]    ]    ]    ]    ]
{    {    {    {    {    }    }    }    }    )
(    (    (    (    (    )    )    )    )    )
[    [    [    (    [    ]    ]    ]    ]    ]
{    {    {    {    {    }    }    }    }    }
```

55

change in time was completely
removed from the vast open space
heated by the edges of plants;
and we were nearly home; talking
on the muddy roadside our bikes
next to us; using those seconds
to rest; not having slept well
in cold tents the night before

: : :

now the box room is the color
of afternoon sunlight projected
through the curtains; a slightly
darker tone than in the morning
and it will reduce more in time;
the change impossible to detect
from moment to moment but as I
sit and work the gradient is
clear; precisely I   calculate
a prediction; that in months
the room will be pitch black
and negative light will pull
the walls in right through me

```
$ brainfuck delta_t.bf

++++++++++
+        +
+        +
+        +
+        +
+        +
+        +
+        +
+        +
++++++++++
+++++++++
+        +
+        +
+        +
+        +
+        +
+        +
+        +
+++++++++
++++++++
+       +
+       +
+       +
+       +
+       +
+       +
++++++++
+++++++
+      +
+      +
+      +
+      +
+      +
+++++++
++++++
+     +
+     +
+     +
+     +
++++++
+++++
+    +
+    +
+    +
+++++
++++
+   +
+   +
++++
+++
+  +
+++
```

57

./code --poetry - A collection of executable art

DESCRIPTION

by_conspiracy_or_design.js *[JavaScript]*   6-7

Are you an art historian prone to seeing the golden spiral
everywhere? Are you sick of the government controlling your
brain from 31,415 feet? Does trigonometry make you want to
sin and tan, just cos? Try JavaScript, for just $16.18. Live
error free and start failing silently. Who cares about
whitespace? Write your own script, with JavaScript.

alphanumeric.jl *[Julia]*   8-9

This code poem was redacted by Julia. The mysterious woman
that gave you hash at that house party last Friday? No, it's
a programming language loved by scientists. What are they
hiding behind all those hashtags? The truth about Bigfoot
and other cryptids is out there, but the fuckers encrypted
it...

divide.php *[PHP]*   10-11

The incredibly insecure PHP has been responsible for
introducing dollar signs to three groups: amateur web
programmers, dot-com-boomers, and hackers. In Bret Easton
Ellis' `American Psycho`, Patrick Bateman tells Daisy he
works in "murders and executions" but she hears "mergers and
acquisitions". When a client takes you to an upscale sushi
restaurant in NYC, tell them you work in PHP.

chernobyl.rkt *[Racket]* 12-13

Racket is part of the Lisp family of programming languages,
where all statements are parenthetical (or bracketed).
Perfect for the lisping, digressive and drunken speech of a
Pripyat resident in the aftermath of the Chernobyl disaster.
In Lisp, code is data. But who controls the data? Moscow, of
course.

cold_cloud.cc *[C++]* 14-15

The efficient, unforgiving nature of C++ has its uses. It
isn't just infrastructure and industry that require sharp
knives. Squares of Perlin noise resemble satellite scans of
a desolate nuclear landscape.

bark.png *[Piet]* 16-17

Esoteric programming languages make it difficult to
accomplish even the smallest tasks. With Piet, instructions
are encoded not as text but as blocks of colour: writing a
program involves clicking and colouring individual pixels.
Here, one block of colour produces one character. Yes, this
is a lot of work for a few words, but the effort is etched
into the bark.

grass.sh *[Bash]* 18-19

If you want your computer to experience synesthesia, the
tool you are looking for is "piping". The | character in
bash takes data from one program, and provides it as the
input to another. Run `grass.sh`, and alongside the visuals
you will hear the sound of your hard drive being "piped"
into your speakers.

How can a play be a program? For a start, characters are
variables, whose value is increased or decreased using
insults or compliments. Loops and branches are transitions
between scenes, and everything else is unlocked by special
phrases. All very clever, novel, and unique - but, I'm
afraid, this play merits more insults than compliments from
the audience.

Perl is the programming language of bohemians: fluid,
quirky, witty, and artful - evoking visions of Linear A and
the bizarre sigils, that surely flicker around Larry Wall's
brain as he wakes up.

Like snow from the mountain, programmers are drawn, as if by
gravity, to "low level" languages like C. There is beauty in
working close to hardware, just as there is in getting close
to nature. Is the haiku a static mass of ice and snow,
frozen in time, or an avalanche caught in a snapshot on its
descent? Is connection to a computer connection to nature?

To be a graduate student is to be in a constant state of
looking ahead, to graduation, career, and family life. The
academic programming language Haskell (found at conferences
across the world) promises a better, richer, more elegant
future. But when you're writing it, the dominant observation
is hardship.

In code, there is an uneasy pairing of the mechanical and
the organic. This reminds us that things in nature are often
the results of simple replicable systems. Hidden inside
`water.c` is a tiny 13 character pseudo random number
generator – not entropic enough for mathematical uses, but
enough to give the impression of randomness. As the weather
comes and goes, the system that produces it doesn't change.
Isn't that comforting?

The J programming language is an attempt to define
mathematical notation with the limited set of ASCII symbols.
For this reason, J code can look like a cat has walked over
the keyboard. But everything looks odd to the uninitiated:
that doesn't mean there isn't something wonderful going on
deep below the surface.

When bats fly near wind turbines, the sudden changes in air
pressure can cause fatal barotrauma to their lungs. This bat
is injured, and on a mechanical respirator – its own iron
lung – driven by a Windows batch file. Does the output it
produces look like damaged lung tissue, a sonar map, or
something else?

Created by Yukihiro Matsumoto and plucked from obscurity
like a lump of corundum from a mine, Ruby is the hipster's
programming language. Is that an elegant, faceted gem, or an
ommatidium (a unit in an insect's eye)? Flies swarm over the
patient like patrons over a new bar called Ommatidium in
Brooklyn. Am I hallucinating? I'm starting to feel an itchy
sensation. It must be the fornication – er, formication.

"People worked harder in the good old days." Like when
Objective C was what they used to program the iPhone. How do
you make Smalltalk with that religious relative, when they
hit you with Proverbs 6:6? "If you must stare at your phone
(how rude!), stop slacking and go to biblegateway.com. No,
I've not heard of 'Langton's ant'. We believe in creationism
in this family."

flocking.go *[Go]*   38-39

Go was developed by Google, but it's unlikely that the
incident this poem describes will be appearing in a Google
Doodle any time soon. What did it resemble more? Flocks of
birds, celestial bodies, or the swarming and merging of so
called "metaballs"?

code_violation.pde *[Processing]*   40-41

When you've queued up overnight to get into Wimbledon, by
early afternoon the next day, the sun can go to your head.
As your eyes shunt from left to right and back again, you
start seeing palindromes everywhere. Monica Seles. Angela
Kerek. "Code violation", utters the umpire. You never
learned to code - you prefer making visual art inspired by
your favourite tennis players. Don't worry: Processing will
serve things up on a Venus Rosewater Dish.

blinds.ante *[Ante]*   42-43

In the programming language Ante, each card encodes an
instruction. The result is overwhelming and impossible to
read for the programmer. Yet, the computer never loses
concentration. It's not interested in how things appear at
face value - it looks only at the cards on the table, like a
poker player with prosopagnosia.

steady_hand_game.bef *[Befunge]*   44-45

If you think programming in 2D is easier than programming
via text, Befunge will disappoint you. In Befunge, a cursor
cruises around the text grid, following the arrows and
running the commands it encounters beneath. What fun
though! After all, how many other languages have a built-in
jump-pad (denoted with #).

clock_in_clock_out.cs *[C#]*   46-47

I wonder how many of the people waiting on this platform are
on their way to a corporate programming gig? Is it a crime
for a job to be well-liked but a little boring at times,
just like C#? This program is self-referential: it prints
random substrings of itself. The dot matrix arrivals board
is glitching. The Circle line goes in circles. Time for a
career change? Any minute now.

firefighting.py *[Python]*   48-49

Everything is clear and accessible when you write programs
in Python. Firelight illuminates the darkness. No, not the
snake, this language is named after Monty Python: are we
witnessing a tragic conflagration and a farce of human
management at the same time?

irc.py *[Python]*   50-51

Internet Relay Chat (IRC) was one of the first internet chat
rooms. Used primarily by hackers, gamers, and a
disproportionate amount of Finns, it's a true artefact of
the old internet. `irc.py` contains a simple Markov chain
that runs on chat logs and produces conversations that are
remarkably real, apart from one aspect: these conversations
are read-only.

fourohfour.erl *[Erlang]*   52-53

404 has achieved a surprising level of notoriety in internet
culture. It's kind of a B-lister compared to, say, 69 or 420
- but on the rise. Perhaps it's already overtaken the
old-timer, 101. If more of the internet was written in the
fault-tolerant yet awkward Erlang, 404 might have had 0
cultural prominence.

stack.lua *[Lua]*   54-55

A fundamental programming rule: each parenthesis must have a
match. Opening and closing in nested trees and sub-tasks - a
valid program always has a start and an end. Is life not
much the same? Is opening, closing, and sorting symbols the
only human endeavour?

delta_t.bf *[Brainfuck]*   56-57

Brainfuck has only six commands: +-<>[]. This makes it easy
to write a poem: every other character is ignored. There is
nothing that can be computed in any other language that
Brainfuck cannot also compute. Don't be deceived - small
incremental steps (when placed in the correct order) are not
linear in their effect.

Many programming languages have a print command such as
`println()` in Julia or `print()` in Python. You can
find examples in this book. These commands tell the
computer to print a message to the console (or
terminal) window. In this book, we've turned the print
command on its head by exploring the artistic potential
of printing code poems and their outputs on paper. The
book you hold in your hands cannot respond to any of
the commands in the code poems. It cannot "print"
anything, yet it is printed. `./code --poetry` can be
seen, in part, as a work of conceptual poetry that asks
the question "what happens when you print a digital
artwork that consists of two inextricably linked
components, a code poem and its output?"

The code poems (what the computer reads), placed on the
left facing pages of this book, translate aesthetic
elements of a screen into print. For example, many
programmers prefer to code on a screen with a dark
background, to reduce eye strain, with coloured text
that highlights particular key words and symbols.
Reading code on a backlit screen with a dark background
is very different to reading a coloured page lit by
another source: a colour looks different in print and
on the web.

Printing the animations (what the computer writes),
presented on the right facing pages of this book,
presents further challenges. On code-poetry.com, the
animations for the code poems play. How can movement be
represented in print? One method would be to present
the animations as a flipbook, with a single page per
frame. In this book, we have instead included
screenshots of the output. Sometimes, a single
screenshot is included, for example for `delta_t.bf`.
For other code poems, multiple screenshots are
presented, for example for `by_conspiracy_or_design.js`
- the reader can assemble a virtual flipbook in their
mind's eye. The animations are presented here with some
artistic licence: a page cannot produce them like a
computer can.

Each code poem is constrained by the vocabulary of its programming language, the computer's demand that it function as a syntactically-valid program, and the requirements of its human readers. This project itself is also fundamentally constrained: a program generates the print book and the dynamic website from a single source. This means that a change to the print version propagates a change to the web version.

Beyond that, a shared style scheme defines the syntax highlighting and formatting of the text for both the print and the web. The design requirements of print and web are different and often contradictory: shapes, colours, sizes, fonts, and spacing cannot be optimally unified across these media. The requirement to define a shared design for both media is an impossible constraint. We hope you enjoy our imperfect solution.

A brief survey of other examples of printed code poetry will help contextualise this book.

`code {poems}`, an anthology edited by Ishac Bertran (Barcelona: Impremta Badia, 2018) includes semantically valid code poems. Some of these code poems produce an output, but none of the outputs are presented in the book. The code poems are printed in black and white.

`Code Poems: 2010-2019` (Minneapolis: Post-Asemic Press, 2020) by Francesco Aprile prints code poems, sometimes in black and white and sometimes with syntax highlighting and a dark background. The outputs of the code poems are not included. However, 'Civil poem 2019' (pp. 1-10) appears to consist of textual output to a console.

Shawn Lawson's trilogy of `Code Poetry` books (author's edition: 2015, 2017 & 2019) collects code poetry created by his students at Rensselaer Polytechnic Institute. In these books, the code poems are printed alongside their outputs, and often with input and output on facing pages.

The outputs are coloured and sometimes take up the
whole page. In the 2017 edition, the outputs are
framed in terminal windows that float above the inputs.
The outputs include screenshots of animations, for
example the output of John Noonan's Processing code
poem on page 37 of the 2017 edition. Thanks to
Krzysztof Siejkowski for bringing Lawson's books to our
attention.

Sy Brand's `code::art` journal (2019-) includes work
by multiple authors. Code poems are printed sometimes
in black and white and sometimes with syntax
highlighting and dark backgrounds. In most cases, the
outputs of code poems, if there are any, are not
included. In Issue 0 (2019), 'over/under' by Alice
Strete presents both input and output on a single page
(p. 3).

For a more detailed contextualisation of this project
in the field of code poetry, see our article: Daniel
Holden and Chris Kerr. "Optimizing code for
performance: reading `./code --poetry`". `Poetry and
Contemporary Visual Culture` / `Lyrik und
zeitgenössische Visuelle Kultur`. Ed. Magdalena Korecka
and Wiebke Vorrath. Berlin/Boston, MA: De Gruyter, 2023
[forthcoming].

With this context in mind, and with gratitude to these
brilliant examples of code poetry, we can state what is
distinctive about `./code --poetry`, with regard to the
print medium. Our project uses a single shared process
to present, in print and online, both the code poem and
its dynamic execution by the computer. The way this
book is printed is constrained by the way the code
poems are presented online, and vice versa.

        Chris

```
       _
       |
       ~


    ,d88b.d88b,
   88888888888
   `Y8888888Y'
     `Y888Y'
       `Y'


!"#$%&'()*+,-./0123456789:;<=>?@
ABCDEFGHIJKLMNOPQRSTUVWXYZ[\]^_`
abcdefghijklmnopqrstuvwxyz{|}~
```

When most people picture the world of programming, they
don't have a very vivid image in mind. Visualising a
programmer sitting down and enjoying some TV in the
evening is easy - imagining what they do all day at
work is something else. It's clear what programmers do
in a physical sense (press keys on a keyboard, click
the mouse, etc.), but what does it feel like to
actually be a programmer?

If this is something you want to understand, perhaps a
good place to start is with programming languages. Very
roughly, programming languages are half-way between
natural languages (such as English) and mathematics.
Like natural languages they have structure and a
vocabulary. And like mathematics they are concise,
specific, and use many unusual words and symbols for
which the meanings must be learned. But once you know a
programming language, the process of actually
commanding the computer is surprisingly simple. You
don't need to learn how to use any complex software:
all you do is write your program in a text file and
open it with another program.

So far so good, until you realise there is no single
programming language - there are thousands, and
programmers may learn dozens over their careers. The
time it takes to learn a new programming language
varies. If the programmer already knows a similar
language it could take a weekend.

If the language is particularly weird and complex, it might take years. And while the most popular programming languages are often taught at university, some programming languages are so obscure that only a handful of people on the planet know them.

The internet has archived hundreds of ancient programming languages - their users long since moved on, retired, or in some cases, simply dead. If you start learning one of these languages today, you may well be the world's number one expert tomorrow.

The richness of this field is one of the many things that makes programming fascinating. It isn't uncommon for programmers to learn new languages in their spare time for fun - and many have dedicated their lives to studying languages and developing their own. Half a century since their invention, programming languages remain the most flexible, powerful instrument in the toolbox of a programmer.

For all these reasons, what programming languages you speak is a significant question in the programming community. It's like asking what country a person is from - it gives a quick insight into their background, many of their thoughts, their opinions and their experiences. And, just like natural languages, programming languages influence the people who speak them - they introduce an implicit culture and a world-view, because it's programming languages that give programmers the vocabulary to describe problems they encounter, and more importantly, their potential solutions.

So people tend to identify with certain languages more than others, which leads to an amplification effect. As people flock to the language that most accurately suits them they homogenise the culture. Borders are drawn, nations grow, and flags are raised.

These factions have been known to engage in "religious wars" about which style of programming is best. Reading the arguments is an experience - somewhere between a theoretical debate between particle physicists and a childhood argument over Porsche vs Ferrari.

So when programmers want to communicate code with each other, choosing a common programming language can be difficult. When the code doesn't need to be run by a computer, often the choice is a language called "Pseudocode" - a kind of Esperanto of the programming world. In other words, an abstract and flexible amalgamation of the most common elements of programming languages, packaged in a sensible, clear syntax to try and ensure there is minimal confusion.

Often, Pseudocode, combined with a bit of mathematics, is enough to get the point across, but not always. Just as Esperanto is undeniably a Euro-centric global language, Pseudocode is an "imperative" style of programming language. There are plenty of communities who don't like that. Similarly, it doesn't matter to a monolingual Chinese speaker if you speak Esperanto or French: they're not going to understand, and half of the information is lost in translation.

In the world of tech we hear a lot about new machines, new businesses, and new personalities, but we hear very little about the quiet cultural revolution that has been happening alongside the development of programming and computer science - a muffled eruption taking place in dark bedrooms, in basements and offices. An eruption of geeks, outcasts, gays, socialists, hippies and anarchists, nerds and libertarians. Much of it has been faceless - echoing only in its own spaces, propagating to the outside world slowly via the internet. On the outside it looks bizarre and impossible to decipher, but on the inside you will find a number of things that have come to unite programmers. A sense of generosity and selflessness, a love of clever and playful things, a wish to remain faceless or anonymous, an absence of financial motivation, and an overarching longing to be accepted. These remain the same regardless of the programming language being spoken.

And there is a good reason to sit up and take notice of this culture which has rumbled away quietly. It will play a large role in the future of humanity. Programming will be taught in secondary school like English and Mathematics, and the experiences of the programmer today will be the model for the experience of many millions of children to come.

If we are interested in showing people how it feels to be a programmer, then we need to know what aesthetic symbols represent programmers - the objects that demonstrate their common experiences and bring them together regardless of faction and creed. These are the stones left over from the destruction of the tower of Babel and each one is an important artefact.

In this archaeological dig, the most significant stone that has been turned over so far are the set of symbols called "ASCII".

ASCII stands for "American Standard Code for Information Interchange", and it is an agreed set of symbols, and their encoding, that allows programmers and computers to communicate textual data. It was developed in the 1960s but has stuck around a long time since then.

There are 95 printable characters specified by ASCII (including the space character). 52 of these characters are the alphabetic characters, 10 are the numerals, and the other 33 are various miscellaneous symbols that largely hold their place thanks to a number of different historical circumstances.

```
!"#$%&'()*+,-./0123456789:;<=>?@
ABCDEFGHIJKLMNOPQRSTUVWXYZ[\]^_`
abcdefghijklmnopqrstuvwxyz{|}~
```

Most lay people may have never used, or even seen, many of the symbols in ASCII before. Characters such as 'pipe' |, 'tilde' ~, 'hash' #, and 'at' @ might all seem very odd things to include (although the latter two are more familiar to people these days thanks to Twitter and Instagram). Equally, many lay people may be just as surprised at some of the omissions. People in the UK might be wondering where the 'pound sign' £ (which sits above the 3 on our keyboards) is?

Japanese people also lack their own currency symbol. They solved this problem by having Japanese software draw the ASCII 'backslash' character \ as a yen symbol ¥ on screen - a decision that has given file paths on Japanese versions of Windows a very expensive look (e.g. C:¥Windows¥Microsoft.NET¥Framework¥').

Programmers, unlike lay people, will know all these ASCII symbols well. This is because programming languages almost exclusively use ASCII symbols to represent code. Programmers typically type hundreds or even thousands of these symbols every day and no single symbol goes without use.

Given that, why then are there symbols for 'plus' +, 'minus' - (a borrowed hyphen) and 'equals' =, but not for multiplication or division? Programmers are forced to use 'asterisk' * to represent multiplication and 'forward slash' / to represent division.

The simple reason for the selection of symbols (anyone who is a little older than me will have already guessed this) is that almost all of the ASCII symbols derive directly from the symbols that were on standard American typewriters of the day.

This at least explains the 'at' symbol @ and the 'hash' symbol #. 'At' was originally intended as a shorthand to signify the price various goods were bought at (e.g. '4 tables @ $128'), and 'hash' was used to represent identifying numbers (e.g. 'shipment #512').

The typewriter also explains another group of symbols that were originally meant to be typed over the top of previous symbols. On a typewriter the backspace key doesn't erase the previous character but moves the paper backward by the width of a space. The accent characters ^, ~ and ` were placed over other letters. The typewriter also explains why the division symbol is missing - previously an approximation was achieved by typing the hyphen character and then the colon : character on top (for multiplication the x character was used). This also explains 'underscore' _. Bold characters could be printed on a typewriter by directly printing the same character two or three times on top of itself but italics were impossible. 'Underscore' was introduced so underlined text could be used as an alternative.

While many of these characters have completely lost their original context and meaning they have gained an entirely new purpose in writing code. For example, 'pipe' | is used to chain a series of commands, and 'tilde' ~ means to flip a set of bits such that zeroes become ones and vice versa. Programmers have been forced to combine symbols in creative ways: putting 'hyphen' - next to 'greater than' > to make 'arrow' ->, putting 'hash' # next to 'exclamation mark' ! to make a symbol called 'she-bang' #!, or putting two 'greater thans' > next to 'equals' = to make an obscure symbol called 'monadic bind' >>= .

The ASCII symbols are a set of symbols that define programming. But they are more than that - they are the words that all programmers have learned to speak and the icons that every programmer has passed their eyes over and muttered the names of long into the night.

ASCII, more than any single programming language, represents the common language of programming culture - the silent, subtle communication that has built so much and allowed thousands of programmers from around the world to slowly, independently, construct a culture.

I've often teased my girlfriend by saying I'm going to get a tattoo of the 95 printable ASCII characters. Her reaction is always the same - an expression which says both "please don't", and "you massive nerd" at the same time. So unofficially, I like to think of this poetry collection as my missing love letter to ASCII - a thank you note to those 95 weird little symbols that have ended up representing my life and the life of many others like me.

/ Dan

Acknowledgements

Many of the code poems in this book appeared in an earlier, self-published version in 2016.

'iron_lung.bat' previously appeared in *Battalion*, a print anthology published by Sidekick Books in 2018. 'alphanumeric.jl', 'an_avalanche_of_stars.c', 'firefighting.py' and 'submarine.ijs' were previously published online by *Welcome to the Jungle* in 2019. Many thanks to the editors. 'bark.png' won the "bend the rules" category in the 2015 Source Code Poetry Competition. Thank you to the judges of this competition.

Many thanks to the following friends for their feedback on drafts of this book: S. J. Fowler, Bob Bright, Susie Campbell, Laura Davis, Ailsa Holland, Stephen Sunderland, Simon Tyrrell, and Martin Wakefield.

Sincere gratitude to Dr Wiebke Vorrath and Magdalena Korecka for their insightful interest in this project.

Finally, special thanks to Aaron Kent and Broken Sleep Books.

```
uppercase_sample = 'LAYOUTYOURUNREST'
lowercase_sample = 'layoutyourunrest'
```

www.ingramcontent.com/pod-product-compliance
Lightning Source LLC
LaVergne TN
LVHW070751060326
832904LV00012BA/306